AutoRacing/USA

1988/The Year in Review

Executive Publisher: W.P. Fred Stevenson

Publisher: Sandra Stevenson

Editor: Leslie Ann Taylor

Photo Editor: Judith V. Stropus

Results Editor: Janet L. Detzel

Copy Editor: James Potter

Typography: Janet Lynn

Advertising & Trade Sales: Stevenson & Brown International, Inc.
Lakeville, Connecticut 06039

Printed By: Hunter Publishing Company
Winston-Salem, North Carolina

Published & Distributed By: Fred Stevenson Publishing, Inc.
Lakeville, Connecticut 06039

Title page photo credits:
Geoffrey Hewitt
David Taylor
David Taylor
Leslie Lovett
Doc Waldrop
Rich Chenet

Contents

Foreword

by GEOFF BRABHAM

*I*N 1988, *THE ELECTRAMOTIVE* Engineering team performed an amazing feat: We captured 10 wins in our Nissan GTP, eight of which came one right after the other. In the process, I won the the IMSA Camel GTP Drivers Championship.

Need I say that my success is owed to the unstinting team work that supported me? From Don Devendorf and his Electramotive crew, to designers Trevor Harris and Yoshi Suzuka, to Kas Kastner, Nissan's national motorsports director, I've witnessed uncommon dedication, talent and determination. It's sheer joy to see hard work pay off.

And, let's not forget John Morton, Tom Gloy and Derek Daly, the kind of co-drivers without whom such points championships would be impossible.

It's not a season I'm soon to forget. But just in case a few of the details should get hazy, I'm delighted and proud to have had our accomplishments chronicled in this superb book. I invite you to join me in remembering quite a year in this sport we all love. Welcome to the sixth volume of *AutoRacing/USA*.

Geoff Brabham

It takes teamwork to make a champion.
Photo/W.H. Murenbeeld.

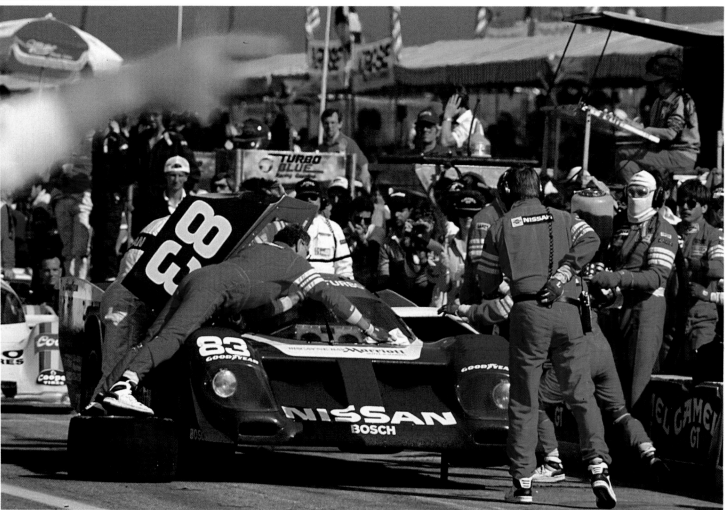

©1988 Volkswagen

What distinguishes the Volkswagens we race from yours.

The parts above are parts we use to modify the Volkswagen GTIs, Golfs, Sciroccos and Foxes we race each motorsports season.

The big object is a roll bar. The smaller ones include a safety net, fire extinguisher, 5-point seatbelt, heavy duty MacPherson struts and a kill switch.

Exotic technology it isn't.

But that's precisely our point.

You see, we've already tested the performance, endurance and reliability of these cars at our testing facilities in Wolfsburg, Germany. The motorsports circuit here in the U.S. is where we prove this technology.

And prove it we do. By competing in classes that require showroom stock cars (with the exception of the parts noted above), we race the very same

Volkswagens you test drive and buy. To us, it's the only way to race.

And so far so good.

Last year, we ended up with six different National Championships under our belt. This season, Volkswagen is leading the Manufacturer's Championship in the IMSA Firestone Firehawk Touring Class.

Now that you've seen the technology that goes into our race Volkswagens, why not see the "stripped down" showroom version at your nearest Volkswagen dealer.

Go for a test drive. That's the best part of all.

German engineering. The Volkswagen way.

Introduction

by LESLIE ANN TAYLOR

AFTER YEARS OF SPENDING more nights in motels located near racetracks than in my own home (or so it seemed), circumstances forced a hiatus and I became a distant observer of auto racing rather than an involved participant. This past season I returned to the circus.

I'm here to tell you, folks, that what I discovered upon my return is really exciting. Oh, the motels are pretty much the same, still charging the same preposterous racers' rates. But there's a vitality permeating the sport of professional auto racing that is invigorating. It seemed that, for a while, the sport overall was stagnant. The track locales were the same, the front-runners were the same, the technology advanced sluggishly or only in response to outrage, the general coverage reflected an unchanging level of mildly bored interest, the spectator numbers grew but then so did the population as a whole, and the too few sponsors represented predictable markets.

How things have changed!

This past season, I worked races at tracks which not only didn't exist in '87, they stopped existing a week after the race was held. The increase in the number of temporary circuits and their impact on both the sport and its fans is addressed by Pete Lyons in his sixth appearance in *AutoRacing/USA*. In his thoughtful, wonderfully crafted analysis of this current trend, Lyons proposes some guidelines which can only benefit all involved...well, perhaps the land speculators will feel their noses a bit out of joint.

I invite you to share a conversation Randy Hallman has with the man who seems to be a friend to all, Bobby Allison. Addressing the fact that Allison has an awful lot of cloudy space in his memory banks, Hallman reviews the '88 Winston Cup season and re-introduces Allison to some of those new front-runners—one of whom is Bobby's own son.

Whether it be perusing David Phillips recap of the Indy car year, delving into Bill Lovell's IMSA reviews, or reading Phil Elliott's summary of the year in drag racing, the technological advances reported on today's race tracks are startling. But Mike Harris makes his debut appearance in *AutoRacing/USA* by probing one area of technology—the ability to immediately and effectively respond to trauma caused by a major racing incident—and finds one area of the sport appallingly lacking.

For an overview of almost all of auto racing's diverse arenas, Dick Berggren presents a comprehensive "State of the Sport" commentary which is guaranteed to rile certain segments of both the fans and participants. Although individual inclinations may color your reading, it is encouraging to share Berggren's reporting of the increase in both the amount and the quality of the coverage auto racing received in 1988, and the health of the sport overall as indicated by improved facilities and the ever-increasing spectator numbers.

The glorious photographs will illustrate the fact that Madison Avenue has suddenly discovered that auto racing fans are interested in more than the traditionally masculine beer, cigarettes and motor oil. This new awareness of the distaff side of the sport has opened the doors to millions of new sponsor dollars. And we're not just talking female fans, friends, although they abound. Andy Hall presents Charlotte/Daytona Dash competitor Shawna Robinson, the first woman to win a NASCAR feature race. Meet the marvelous Patty Moise, no stranger to ARCA pole positions, and one of drag racing's most exciting new talents, Lori Johns.

As I say, there's a new excitement enveloping American professional auto racing. The words and images comprising *AutoRacing/USA* portray this vitalizing energy, capturing the 1988 season with its glories and heartbreaks, magic and misery.

I hope you'll enjoy our sixth presentation of *AutoRacing/USA*, the year in review. It's good to be back.

When everyone drives one great car, the winner is one great driver.

Bruce Feldman: Barber-Saab Pro Series Champion

The Barber-Saab Pro Series was conceived to test and display the skills of emerging driving stars, rather than merely plumb the depths of their pockets.

And the wisdom of this concept has produced exciting competition. This year, the championship wasn't decided until the 12th and final race of the series, at Florida's Tamiami Park. There, Bruce Feldman made good on his three years Barber-Saab Pro Series experience and the confidence shown by his sponsor—Fluid Systems—to edge out the competition and drive off with a new Saab Turbo.

Saab congratulates all 53 drivers who drove one great car in pursuit of driving greatness. And we look forward to more of the same in the 1989 Barber-Saab Pro Series.

SAAB
The most intelligent cars ever built.

WE TRAVEL WITH A FAST CROWD

ESPN'S MOTOR SPORTS COVERAGE. THE MOST COMPREHENSIVE SCHEDULE EVER.

Throughout 1989, ESPN® will bring you in-depth coverage of more than 200 events from around the world, featuring Formula 1, NASCAR, CART, IMSA and much more. And our weekly series "SpeedWeek,™" and "Motorweek Illustrated™" provide an insider's perspective on all the action on and off the track.

So, when you want to get around with the fast crowd, turn to ESPN.

1989 AUTO RACING HIGHLIGHTS

3/5	NASCAR GoodWrench 500	8/13	F1 Hungarian Grand Prix
3/26	F1 Brazilian Grand Prix	8/13	NASCAR—The Budweiser At The Glen
4/2	NASCAR TranSouth 500	8/20	NASCAR Champion Spark Plug 400
4/9	NASCAR Valleydale Meats 500	8/26	NASCAR Busch 500
4/16	NASCAR First Union Bank 400	8/27	F1 Belgian Grand Prix
4/24	F1 San Marino Grand Prix	9/3	NASCAR Southern 500
5/7	NASCAR Winston 500	9/10	F1 Italian Grand Prix
5/29	IMSA GTP Series: Lime Rock	9/10	CART Road America 200
6/4	NASCAR Budweiser 500	9/17	NASCAR Delaware 500
6/11	NASCAR Sears Point	9/25	F1 Grand Prix of Portugal
6/25	CART Budweiser/G.I. Joe's 200	10/1	NASCAR Holly Farms 400
7/2	IMSA GTP Series: Watkins Glen, New York	10/1	F1 Spanish Grand Prix
		10/22	NASCAR A.C. Delco 500
7/2	CART Cleveland Grand Prix	10/22	Japanese Grand Prix
7/9	F1 French Grand Prix	11/5	F1 Australian Grand Prix
7/16	F1 British Grand Prix	11/19	NASCAR Atlanta Journal 500
7/30	F1 German Grand Prix	PLUS Coverage of NHRA, Off Road and Rally USAC	
7/30	IMSA GTP Series: Portland, Ore.		

IF YOU LIKE TO DRIVE FAST, WE HAVE A PROGRAM FOR YOU.

Skip Barber Racing School

Learn to race at the school the pros choose.

Graduates include one third of the starting field at last year's Indianapolis 500.

Your classrooms – The great race tracks of North America.

Your textbooks – State-of-the-art Formula Fords.

Skip Barber Formula Ford Race Series

The ideal way to experience the challenge of open wheel competition. We provide all cars, preparation, and transport.

Your job is to drive – The fun part of racing.

Barber/Saab Pro Series

The ultimate, IROC-style Professional series for turbo-charged, open-wheel race cars. 160 mph top speeds. Twelve races, each run with a major event. National television coverage. Prize money: $35,000 per race.

BMW/Skip Barber Advanced Driving School

Designed for the serious driver who wants to extract the most from his or her performance automobile.

Featuring the exciting new BMW M-3, the School takes you step-by-step through each phase of performance driving, from theory through practical applications.

The emphasis is on <u>driving technique</u>, not racing.

Entrants in the Barber Saab Pro Series require previous race experience.

For a free brochure on the Skip Barber Program of your choice, call (203) 824-0771 or write: The Skip Barber Racing School, Route 7, Canaan, CT 06018. West of the Rockies call: 1 (800) 722-7223.

SKIP BARBER RACING SCHOOL

Skip Barber programs are held at these great race circuits.
Brainerd/Bridgehampton/Indianapolis Raceway Park/Lime Rock/Mid-Ohio/Moroso/Pocono/
Riverside/Road America/Road Atlanta/Savannah/Sebring/Waterford Hills/Willow Springs

Commentary: 1988 WAS RACING'S BIGGEST YEAR

by **DICK BERGGREN**
EDITOR, *STOCK CAR RACING & OPEN WHEEL*

*T*HESE ARE BOOM TIMES for big league auto racing. If it ran on an oval in 1988 and if it was a major event, chances are it was sold out.

NASCAR Winston Cup racing came out as the biggest winner. At every stop on the Winston Cup circuit, speedway operators were busy adding new seats, improving their facilities, or, in one case, completely rebuilding the place.

Daytona opened the oval season with an enormously popular win by Bobby Allison in the Daytona 500. In storybook fashion, Bobby was followed across the stripe by his son Davey, who was driving a car that had been wrecked in the final practice session the previous afternoon. High rollers and favored press watched the race from a huge new suite perched above the Winston Tower. The new facility is so high up in the air, it's not only possible to see every inch of the race track, it's even possible to see the Atlantic Ocean several miles away.

As the tour moved from track to track, spectators and drivers were treated to improvements in physical facilities. New grandstands were erected (and immediately sold out) at Dover, Martinsville, Wilkesboro, and Bristol. At North Wilkesboro, the pits were completely revamped and a new garage area was constructed. Rockingham's entrance got an attractive face-lift. Pocono's facilities for drivers and their wives were dramatically improved. Between its February 21 event and its September 11 event, Richmond Speedway's grey old Fairgrounds Raceway was destroyed and replaced by a glittering new palace of speed.

Phoenix was added to the schedule and the first ever Winston Cup race held in Arizona brought the biggest crowd ever to the track. Promoter Buddy Jobe explained that he sunk $5 million into the place in order to get the date.

Of the world's major leagues of auto racing, none emerged with a better balance sheet and better health than NASCAR's Winston Cup. Race after race featured dozens of lead changes. Races were typically won by less than a car length. And the cast of characters—Earnhardt, Waltrip, Elliott, Rudd, Bonnett, Bodine, Allison—who populate the front of NASCAR's pack are not only popular with fans, they make good press.

NASCAR drew more spectators to their Winston Cup events than any other league in the world drew to theirs. The popularity of this series is due to the simple fact that it produces the most exciting, colorful and close competition of any series running. Drivers work their way through the ranks to participate in the Cup. The result is that the very best filter to the top, producing incredible competition.

* * *

CART also drew excellent crowds although its car counts were well down in 1988. The sudden emergence of the Chevrolet racing engine as the dominant force in the series served the Penske team well. But Chevy's success was a demoralizing, even defeating, blow to those teams—and they are in the majority—for whom a Chevrolet racing engine is but a whispy dream. There were a limited number of Chevy engines and they weren't available to all who wanted and could afford them.

As CART drivers—those without the Chevy— complained that it was virtually impossible to win without a Chevy engine, CART's governing body was populated by those with the high-output powerplants in their cars. Those who respond to the rules instead of writing them were a lap down, running something else that most admitted couldn't beat a Chevy. When the year finished, all but one race went to Chevy motors and the champion, Danny Sullivan, was one of the Chevy drivers. The Indianapolis 500 was won by Rick Mears whose car was powered by a Chevrolet.

* * *

America finished another racing season without a world class road racing series. Despite all the venues for road racing, nothing draws consistently big crowds, fields or sponsors in a series that turns left and right in the USA.

* * *

"THANKS TO YOU, MY LIFE'S A WRECK."

"And it's all because you don't take a couple of seconds to buckle your safety belt. Listen, it doesn't take a genius to figure out that safety belts save lives. So stop destroying my life. Buckle up. Please."

YOU COULD LEARN A LOT FROM A DUMMY. BUCKLE YOUR SAFETY BELT.

A Public Service Message  Ad Council U.S. Department of Transportation

Saab's 16-valve, turbocharged, twin-overhead cam, fuel-injected powerplant in action.

Ditto.

The closest you'll come to the racing engines of most car companies is in their advertising. Not their showrooms.

Saab, on the other hand, doesn't believe it's right to boast about an engine unless customers can buy it.

The Saab Turbo that powers Skip Barber's Pro Series cars is the same basic engine you'll find in every Saab 9000 Turbo.

It's the same engine that set 21 international and two world records for speed and endurance.

To test drive the Saab Turbo, visit a Saab showroom. After all, that's a car company's real proving ground.

SAAB
The most intelligent cars ever built.

Sprint car racing experienced a turbulent season. The major consistent element of the year was its biggest winner, Steve Kinser, who once again emerged with the WoO title (his ninth in the club's 11 year history) and more WoO money ($373,900) than anyone else. Kinser even won the first point title for the new USA club.

Even doubters who cling to images of an earlier age were this year persuaded that Steve Kinser just might be the best sprint car driver of all time.

Yet 1988 produced cracks in the foundation of big league sprint car racing. The World of Outlaws, for 10 years the focus of growth in purses and the producer of the best races anywhere in the country, found itself faced with competition for the first time since its founding.

The United Sprint Association (USA) was founded by influential car owners, successful and popular drivers and some disgruntled former WoO officials. Their first events were staged in the fall of 1988 and they brought excellent car counts, races as good as those of the WoO (because they had the same cars and drivers as WoO), and a $100,000 point fund for only three events. In 1989, the USA will go head-to-head against WoO on a regular basis.

There is concern that fields will be split and that seldom, if ever, will fans see all the flat-out types in one field. Both Sammy Swindell and Steve Kinser, the only two champions the WoO has ever known, are investors in USA and will run the USA races in '89. WoO founder Ted Johnson says if Sammy and Steve quit the tour, that's OK because they are so good that they discourage others from participating. Johnson is keeping his chin up while those who raced to national fame—and no small fortune—in his club try to kick his feet out from under him.

Nineteen-eighty-eight just may go down as the last great year in big-time sprint car racing for some time to come.

* * *

The growth of big-time auto racing is partly credited to television exposure. In 1988, there were no fewer than four weekly racing TV magazines: *On Pit Road, Motorweek Illustrated, Speedweek,* and *Inside Winston Cup.* Every CART and Winston Cup event was televised. ESPN led all others in race programming, broadcasting a staggering 209 motorsports events. About one-third of these were done live. In all, ESPN broadcast (including re-airs) over 870 hours of automotive competition during 1988, far more than any network in history. In 1989, ESPN will expand its coverage.

Not only is there more television, it really got good in 1988. Even ABC, which has been consistently criticized for its effort (or lack thereof) seemed to gather itself up and did a splendid job—its best ever—with its premier program, the Indy 500.

In-car cameras pictured everything from drivers winning, to crashing out of the Indy 500, to the angry gestures of drivers who lost the conflict. The in-car cameras gave viewers the most intimate look ever at auto racing.

Fortunately for auto racing, the closer fans got to the sport, the better they liked it.

The networks have copied the best of each other's ideas and established both a video and format technology that makes even a five-hour telecast on the longest stock car race a pleasurable view.

There is certainly room for growth in television. Ken Squier, of *Motorweek,* CBS and WTBS, has been in the front lines of both technical and programming improvements in TV's coverage of racing. His best stuff gets unpacked at his biggest telecast, the Daytona 500, where he first introduced the in-car camera, the face cam, bumper cameras, and in-car radios. So long as Squier's creative genius is allowed liberty, as long as the rest continue to copy that genius, the quality of televised auto racing will improve. As it does, the sport's growth will be fertilized.

Sponsors, without whom there would be far less money to play with and therefore far less of a sport, thrive on television far more than print and radio. They count the every mention and every clear image of their product much as a child counts the size of his marble collection. As the televised base of racing expands, the money flowing into racing will expand, too.

* * *

There was a down-side to the '88 season, however.

Bobby Allison suffered a terrible crash in June at Pocono and was grievously injured. Sprint car racer Brad Doty suffered a broken back in a vicious Eldora crash in July and was paralyzed. As is the case every season, several short track racers lost their lives in minor league events. Sheldon Kinser and Alex Morales lost their battles with cancer. Al Holbert was killed in a private plane crash as was Jon Woodner.

If there was any other down side to 1988, it was in the closing of several of the nation's best short tracks. Real estate values rose so high that the ground under many speedways became more valuable when used for almost anything else other than a race track. Thus, Baylands, whose fans sat in grandstands purchased from the late Ontario Motor Speedway, hosted its last show in 1988, as did the venerable half-mile in Nazareth, Pennsylvania.

So, too, went the legendary Riverside International Raceway as it was finally bulldozed to make room for more houses in the desert of Los Angeles suburbs.

Many more circuits are threatened, including Ascot, whose real estate value may exceed the annual salaries of all the world's professional drivers—including the F1 guys who earn more than $5 million a year.

It is indeed ironic that in racing's best year, some of the best attended and best managed tracks went under. Fortunately, several new tracks are under construction. Heartland in Topeka and a new mile oval in New Hampshire are both very likely to open in 1989.

* * *

As is the case every season, the cars went faster and faster. In NASCAR, a tire war led Goodyear to stop making consistent tires that lasted and to make, instead, fast tires which could compete with rival Hoosier. The result was a dramatic increase in speed and many tire failures with both brands.

The Chevrolet racing engine and new PC17 racing car led the list of technological improvements in Indy car racing.

New body styles provided better aerodynamic downforce in the dirt modifieds of the Northeast while their pavement contemporaries remained mired in seas of discontent. Super Modified racing has technologically stagnated, producing an abundant inventory of cars and parts, leading to the best year Super Modified racing ever had—except on the West Coast where technological development outstripped car owners' ability to pay for it.

New materials for brake pads improved stopping power in all circuits.

* * *

Nineteen-eighty-eight goes down as a big one. Racing earned more exposure on television, in newspapers and magazines than ever before. More sponsors spent more money. More fans than ever before paid to see the competition for themselves. Given America's continuing stable economy, plenty of fuel and the continued growth of interest in racing, 1989 has an odds-on shot of being even bigger that '88.

Equal cars powered by Saab engines, and equipped with Goodyear racing slicks for the first time, resulted in tight competition and record-shattering speeds in all 12 races. Photo/David Lubman.

The Barber Saab Pro Series champion for 1988, Bruce Feldman. Photo/Sidell Tilghman-Courtesy of Saab.

Feldman snatched the title from John Cochran by a mere two points, winning two races and DNFing in two. Photo/Sidell Tilghman-Courtesy of Saab.

IMSA/Barber Saab Pro Series

by ADAM SAAL

MORE *POWERFUL SAAB* Turbo engines and new Goodyear Eagle racing slicks lured a full field of 31 competitors to the Barber Saab season-opener at Miami in February. A win from the pole by Colombia's John Estupinan and a second place showing from Italy's Giuseppe Cipriani made it clear the international contingent meant business in '88.

Indeed, international drivers won nine of the 12 Barber Saab events with Canadian Jeremy Dale, and European Formula Three veteran Harald Huysman, from Oslo, Norway, leading the foreign ranks with three victories each. Huysman's first win came in his American debut in Round Two at Road Atlanta.

Freddie Spencer, three-time World Grand Prix Road Racing champion on motorcycles, made his pro auto racing debut at Del Mar, placing fourth. Photo/Sidell Tilghman-Courtesy of Saab.

Kicking up dirt in the attempt, Bob Dotson takes Randy Harris on the inside. Photo/Ken Brown-Competition Photographers.

Huysman set a new track record in his Hydro Aluminum car to win the pole in Round Three at West Palm Beach only to hit the wall while leading early in the race. Veteran Bruce Feldman of Mawah, New Jersey then slipped by Mark Jaremko, from Spokane, Washington, and crossed the finish line for his first '88 win. Although unspoken, Feldman had quietly determined not to repeat his '87 Series runner-up performance.

Dominant in victory at Round Four at Lime Rock Park was 27-year-old Tom Dolan from Portsmouth, New Hampshire, who went wire-to-wire from the pole in his SoftPro/Famiglia Pasta machine. In Round Five at Mid-Ohio, Dale grabbed the lead at the start and held on to the finish. Feldman took second and the points lead from Estupinan. Formula Three veteran Rob Wilson, a New Zealander now living in Brentford, England, gave an indication of things to come by edging Huysman for third in his American debut.

Second in the championship went to Newport, Rhode Island's John Cochran. He never won a race! Photo/Ken Brown-Competition Photographers.

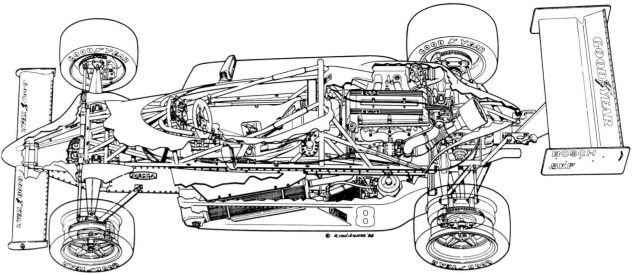

At Watkins Glen Feldman became the season's first repeat winner padding his points lead with a flag-to-flag victory from the pole in his Fluid Systems Barber Saab.

Wilson, in his Goldline Bearings/MOMO Barber Saab, claimed his first U.S. victory in Round Seven at Road America as Cochran took firm hold of second in the point standings with another runner-up showing. Huysman returned to his winning ways during the Series' West Coast swing scoring back-to-back wins—both from the pole—at Portland and Sears Point. The victories moved Huysman past Cochran for second in points.

Dale, splitting his racing time between Barber Saab and IMSA Firehawk, returned at San Antonio with Builders Square sponsorship and won his second race in

The Barber Saab Pro Series race cars are built by Mondiale in Northern Ireland, and resemble Indy-type cars in looks and technology. The turbocharged, 16-valve, 2-liter, twin-cam engine is the same power plant found in Saab 900 and 9000 Turbo Series passenger cars. Photo/Courtesy of Saab.

Tom Dolan sat on the pole and took the win at Lime Rock, but a difficult season brought him only an eighth in the standings. Photo/Randy McKee.

An off-course excursion at Watkins Glen put out Mike Strawbridge after only six laps. Photo/Tom Bernhardt.

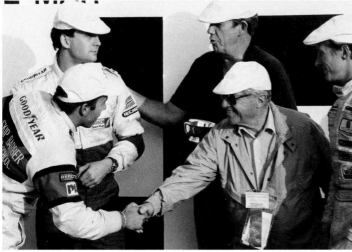

The Del Mar top three (Jeremy Dale, Huysman and Cochran) are congratulated by Vasek Polak and Saab-Scania's Sten Helling. Photo/Sidell Tilghman-Courtesy of Saab.

Norway's Harald Huysman tied with Jeremy Dale for the most wins (three), rounding out the top three in the standings. Photo/Ken Brown-Competition Photographers.

four starts. Cochran's Byron Plantation/Body Glove machine filled the Canadian's mirrors to the finish. Huysman breathed new life to his championship bid with a second place at Del Mar as Dale won his second in a row and third in five starts.

At Tamiami, pole-sitter Wilson led from the start with Cochran slipping by Feldman for second as the green flag dropped. Huysman then passed Feldman for third, only to have the points leader retake the position with a self-described "hold your breath pass" on the pit straight with minutes to go. As Wilson barely edged Cochran for the win, Feldman won the championship with a third place finish. His 115 points led runner-up Cochran's tally of 110. Huysman finished third with 105 points.

Justin Bell ran three races under the supervision of his dad, World Endurance Champion Derek Bell. His best finish was a seventh at Tamiami. Photo/Sidell Tilghman-Courtesy of Saab.

SCCA/Formula Atlantic

by **JOHN ZIMMERMANN**
EDITOR, *SPORTS CAR*

ALTHOUGH *BOTH SCCA* Formula Atlantic series enjoyed fiercely competitive seasons, the topic dominating paddock conversations across the land was the agreement reached with Toyota for the Japanese manufacturer's 1600cc Twin Cam four-cylinder to become Atlantic's designated engine. On the track the two championships started out with pre-season favorites and eventual champions winning, but then turned in different directions.

In the Western Formula Atlantic Championship, former ski racer Dean Hall, runner-up to titlist Johnny O'Connell in '87, started with three straight wins to grab a point lead he never relinquished. In all, Hall won five of the first seven WFA races with his Mike Hartgraves-prepared CB Sports/Ski Optiks Swift. He clinched the title with second place in the eighth event, having recorded five poles and an equal number of fastest race laps to go with his quintet of victories.

Hall's primary opposition materialized only late in the year, when rookie drivers Mitch Thieman and Hiro Matsushita developed into true challengers. Twenty-year-old Thieman earned Rookie of the Year honors and second in the championship, finishing outside the top three only thrice, taking two wins, three poles and two fastest laps. Panasonic heir Matsushita claimed third in points with one win and six other top-four finishes.

The 1988 Western Formula Atlantic champion, Dean Hall. Photo/Gerald Schallie.

Steve Shelton, the 1988 HFC Formula Atlantic Challenge champion. Photo/Courtesy of Sugar Creek Productions.

Dean Hall clinched the Western Formula Atlantic championship, having recorded five poles and an equal number of fastest race laps to go with his quintet of victories. Photo/Gerald Schallie.

The only other drivers to win races were O'Connell, who took a win and a second in three races with Riley Hopkins' five-year-old Ralt RT-4, and former Sports 2000 champion Rod Granberry whose promising season was cut short by a hearing disorder that forced him into premature retirement.

In the East's HFC Formula Atlantic Challenge, Florida car dealer Steve Shelton won the season opener at Road Atlanta, but didn't win again until round seven at Mid-Ohio on Labor Day. A return to Mid-Ohio three weeks later produced similar results, allowing him to clinch the championship the following month in St. Petersburg.

Rookie Colin Trueman, son of the late Indy car owner Jim Trueman, won two straight races, but finished only fifth in points. Photo/Werner Fritz.

Added to Florida car dealer Steve Shelton's three wins in the East were an equal number of fastest race laps and seven pole positions, bringing his record-breaking career total to 14, which tops Gilles Villeneuve's previous mark by one. Photo/Sidell Tilghman.

Amlin, Ohio's Colin Trueman drove a TrueSports-backed Swift. Photo/Gene"Roz"Rosintoski.

J. O. Cunningham won Milwaukee, the first oval race in Atlantic history, then came in first again at St. Pete. He garnered second place in the championship. Photo/Stan Clinton.

Like Hall, his series' runner-up in '87, Shelton produced a season with the Stuart Moore Racing-run Justin Entertainment/AGIP Swift that left him outside the top four only twice—once when a broken stub axle dropped him from an eight-second lead with seven laps to run. Added to his three wins were an equal number of fastest race laps and seven pole positions. The three '88 wins brought his record breaking career total to 14, topping Gilles Villeneuve's previous mark by one.

Shelton didn't cruise to the title, however, as the mid-season point leader had been rookie Colin Trueman in the Budweiser Swift. Colin won two straight races to top the points, but the TrueSports squad seemed to lose the combination after that and he finished only fifth in the championship.

Jocko Cunningham and Scott Harrington ran second and third in the points, each winning one of the year's most significant races and adding another to join Trueman as double winners. Cunningham won Milwaukee, the first oval race in Atlantic history, while Harrington claimed the prestigious GP-supporting round in Montreal—the only Ralt win all year aside from O'Connell's Spokane triumph. The remaining race was taken in fine style by Freddy Rhemrev, who benefited from Shelton's stub axle failure at Lime Rock.

Winning twice, Scott Harrington finished third for the season in the East. Photo/Stan Clinton.

Rookie of the Year honors and a second in the Western Championship went to Mitch Thieman. Thieman scored two wins, three poles and two fastest laps. Photo/Gerald Schallie.

Rookie driver and Panasonic heir Hiro Matsushita claimed third in Western points with one win and six other top-four finishes. Photo/Gerald Schallie.

Robbie Buhl (#30) leads the pack at Road Atlanta. The topic dominating paddock talk in '88 was the agreement reached with Toyota for the Japanese manufacturer's 1600cc Twin Cam four-cylinder to become the series' designated engine in '89. Photo/Gene"Roz"Rostintoski.

Not only did he score his third straight Detroit triumph, Ayrton Senna equalled the all-time record held by Stirling Moss and Niki Lauda by taking his sixth consecutive pole of the year.
Photo/Al Steinberg.

Ayrton Senna qualified his Honda-powered Marlboro McLaren on the pole, then won another humdrum Detroit Grand Prix nearly 40 seconds over teammate Alain Prost.
Photo/Steve Mohlenkamp.

Alain Prost set the fastest lap by chasing down the Ferraris of Gerhard Berger and Michele Alboreto to take over second place until the finish.
Photo/Geoffrey Hewitt.

Driving a normally-aspirated Cosworth V8 to that engine's highest placing, Belgian Thierry Boutsen was third, one lap down. Photo/Steve Mohlenkamp.

France's Alain Prost at speed. Photo/Bob Brodbeck.

The ubiquitous Brazilian fans reveled in countryman Senna's victory. Photo/Al Steinberg.

Gerhard Berger's (#28) dynamite start held a promise for an exciting battle to come, but the McLaren-Honda's dominance spoiled any chances for a Ferrari win. Photo/Steve Mohlenkamp.

SCCA/Valvoline Championship For Bosch/VW Super Vee

by JOHN ZIMMERMANN
EDITOR, *SPORTS CAR*

*F*OR 18 YEARS THE ROBERT Bosch Corporation and Volkswagen have provided young drivers a stage on which to perform, and an audience upon which to make an impression. The result has been a string of champions who've progressed to careers in the upper echelons of the sport.

Added to that list in 1988 was 23-year-old Californian Ken Murillo who moved into the SCCA's Valvoline Championship for Bosch/VW Super Vees after winning the Barber Saab series in 1987. Murillo's season was run on a shoestring-budgeted, race-to-race basis under the careful eye of crew chief Lee Hagen who'd previously guided Arie Luyendyk (1984) and Ken Johnson (1985) to the title.

Ken's quest opened at Phoenix, where his first race in the formula and his first race on an oval produced a first Super Vee victory. With it came a point lead he never relinquished on the way to setting a new record for points earned in a season. The closest he came to losing the lead was at mid-season, when New Zealand's Paul Radisich rode an early summer hot streak to three straight wins and climbed to within a single point.

Ken Murillo, the 1988 Super Vee champion. Photo/Werner Fritz.

Murillo won the Barber Saab series in '87 then moved into Super Vee. His season was run on a shoestring-budgeted, race-to-race basis. Photo/Ken Brown-Competition Photographers.

A crash at the next round, held at the Meadowlands, dropped Radisich back, however, and when Murillo won the following race at Mid-Ohio the die was cast. In the season's final four races Murillo collected three seconds and a win at Nazareth that salted away the title. Over the course of the year he finished lower than fourth only once—sixth at Milwaukee!

Although only fourth in the final tally, Kiwi Radisich provided Murillo's main opposition, taking five poles and three fastest race laps on his way to four victories. Paul showed excellent pace with both Brian Robertson's works Ralt American entry (winner at Long Beach) and Dave Conti's Conproco Ralt (victorious at Detroit, Niagara Falls and Cleveland). However, despite finishing outside the top 10 only twice, Radisich could not match Murillo's point-gathering consistency.

One who nearly did was championship runner-up E.J. Lenzi. Except for a miserable weekend at Long Beach where he qualified 22nd and finished 29th, the Chicago restaurateur was always in the hunt, picking up five seconds, a pair of thirds and a trio of fourths. Victory, however, remained elusive for Lenzi's Peter Jacob-prepared Turtle Wax Ralt, and E.J. was forced to settle for second best.

Third in the standings was Belgian-born Mexican Bernard Jourdain with a pair of victories (Dallas and St. Petersburg) and top five finishes in all but three races. Crashes at Phoenix and the Meadowlands, however, hampered his title hopes.

E. J. Lenzi of Chicago won no races, but placed second five times to take a second in the championship.
Photo/Werner Fritz.

Mike Smith (#34) climbed atop a wayward Bernard Jourdain at the Meadowlands race. Duane May (#21) slipped by, avoiding the tangle.
Photo/Ken Brown-Competition Photographers.

Except for a miserable weekend at Long Beach, restaurateur Lenzi was always in the hunt in his Peter Jacob-prepared Ralt.
Photo/Jim Hatfield.

Fifth place was taken by young Californian Robert Groff, whose exuberant pace with his family-run Ralt produced a quartet of pole positions, a trio of fastest race laps and wins at Milwaukee and Road America. Four finishes outside the top 10 doomed his championship dream.

The only other drivers to win races were Oregon's Smith brothers, Mark and Mike. Mark (sixth in the final points) took top honors at the Meadowlands with his Dave White Motorsports Ralt, while Mike (seventh) won at Indianapolis Raceway Park with his Evergreen Aviation-backed Ralt American entry.

From Northridge, California, ARS driver Mike's younger brother, Bob Groff. Photo/Steve Mohlenkamp.

New Zealand's Paul Radisich rode an early-summer hot streak to three straight wins, totaling four for the year, placing fourth in points. Photo/Geoffrey Hewitt.

Bob Groff won twice, sat on the pole four times, and had three fastest laps, to finish fifth in points. Photo/Steve Mohlenkamp.

Richard DeLorto took a short flight after colliding with Michael Dow at Detroit. *Photo/Al Steinberg.*

Bernard Jourdain. *Photo/Steve Mohlenkamp.*

Third in the standings was Belgian-born Mexican Bernard Jourdain with a pair of victories and top-five finishes in all but three races. Crashes at Phoenix and the Meadowlands, however, hampered his title hopes. Photo/Steve Mohlenkamp.

CART/HFC American Racing Series

by DAVID PHILLIPS
CART EDITOR, *ON TRACK/MOTORING NEWS*

WITH *FINANCIAL SUPPORT* from the Household Finance Corporation, the American Racing Series (ARS) continued its steady, if frustratingly slow, development in 1988. Although the average number of entries continued to hover between 15 and 18, the competition was considerably deeper than in the first two seasons of the ARS. It was not until Jon Beekhuis' Labor Day-weekend win at Mid-Ohio, in fact, that there was a repeat winner and by season's end, a total of seven different drivers had wins in the 12-race series.

The ARS title boiled down to a four-way battle between Beekhuis, Tommy Byrne, Dave Simpson, and Calvin Fish. Beekhuis, a 28-year-old native of Salinas, California, operated from race to race on a wing and a prayer, before finally clinching the title in the final race at Miami. Byrne, another who seldom knew if he would be racing from one event to the next, also won twice and fell a mere three points shy of the title. The consistent Simpson, who won at Milwaukee, missed the final two events after suffering injuries in his Winston Cup debut. Fish was repeatedly let down by mechanical problems but scored two close wins at Toronto and Nazareth. Although he didn't compete often enough to figure in the title race, Juan Manuel Fangio II—nephew and namesake of the five-time Argentine world champion—drove brilliantly and matched Beekhuis, Byrne and Fish with two wins.

Jon Beekhuis drove two different cars to the 1988 American Racing Series championship. Photos/Al Steinberg (below), Stan Clinton (bottom).

Dave Simpson won at Milwaukee but missed the final two events after suffering injuries in his Winston Cup debut, yet still finished third in points. Photo/Ron McQueeney.

Juan Manuel Fangio II (#12) ran a limited season, but drove brilliantly to match the two wins of Beekhuis, Byrne and Fish. Here, he attempts to take Fish on the inside. Photo/Werner Fritz.

Calvin Fish was repeatedly let down by mechanical problems but scored two close wins at Toronto and Nazareth, ending up fourth for the year. His team owner is Molly Shierson, daughter of CART car owner Doug Shierson. Photo/Ken Brown-Competition Photographers.

Tommy Byrne won twice, but fell three points shy of the title. Photo/Art Flores.

The Buick V6 engine powers each of the Wildcat Marches driven in the American Racing Series. Photo/Ken Brown-Competition Photographers.

CART/PPG Indy Car World Series

by **David Phillips**
CART EDITOR, *ON TRACK/MOTORING NEWS*

"MAN'S *REACH MUST* exceed his grasp,"** wrote Robert Browning, "Or what's a heaven for?" Few would deny that Penske Racing's reach exceeded its grasp for the past two seasons when the development of the Ilmor-Chevrolet engine and the unloved PC-15 and -16 chassis relegated Rick Mears, Danny Sullivan and occasional third man Al Unser to cameo roles in victory lane. In 1988, however, the Chevy proved virtually unbeatable and the Nigel Bennett-designed Penske PC-17 chassis was the envy of CART. As a result, Sullivan swept to nine poles, four wins and the CART/PPG Indy Car World Series title while Mears had to "settle" for his third Indy 500 win.

The dominant force of 1988 was neither a team, driver, or chassis, however, but the Ilmor-Chevrolet engine. All told, the Chevy won 14 of 15 poles, 14 of 15 races and led an astounding 1,911 of the year's 2,112 laps.

Following their fast but unreliable 1987 season, Mario Andretti and Newman/Haas Racing began the year as consensus favorites. And Mario opened the year with a resounding victory. Yet those who witnessed Mears demolish the field until his race-ending tangle with Randy Lewis on lap 23, knew the Pennzoil PC-17 would have taken some catching on that day. From half-distance, Mario cruised home to his 50th career Indy car win ahead of the resurgent Roberto Guerrero (driving what would be his only truly competitive race of the year in his first Indy car start since his horrific accident in September, 1987).

Danny Sullivan swept to nine poles and four wins to earn the 1988 CART/PPG Indy Car World Series championship, his first. Photo/Taylors Photography.

At Toronto, Sullivan claimed his third consecutive pole, but it was Al Unser, Jr. who celebrated the victory. Danny was second, Michael Andretti third. Photo/David Taylor.

It took six years, but Danny finally made it to the top in CART. Photo/Bill Stahl.

Sullivan, in the Miller High Life Penske PC-17, became the third driver to win $1 million in a single season, joining teammate Rick Mears and Bobby Rahal. Photo/Rich Chenet.

Al Jr. and the Galles team got their race setup perfect at Toronto, scoring Al's second of four wins for the year. "Little Al" drove one of five cars on the circuit powered by the unbeatable Ilmor-Chevrolet engine, but was handicapped by the problematic March 88C chassis. Photo/Stan Clinton.

If Phoenix offered proof of the PC-17's oval track prowess, Long Beach confirmed its street smarts—at least in practice and qualifying. For although Danny Sullivan hustled his Miller High Life machine to the pole, the race was an entirely different matter. Unser, Jr. sliced past Andretti into the lead by the end of the first lap. From there on, Al was in a class by himself. When a muffed pit stop cost him the lead, Al reloaded and tracked down the leaders, pulling to a half-lap lead, leaving second place to a thrilling dice between Kevin Cogan and Rahal. Unser finally crossed the line more than a lap ahead of Rahal after Cogan's thirsty Schaefer/Machinists Union March was forced to make a third fuel stop.

As always, the month of May at Indy takes the form of a three act play of sorts, beginning with the first two weeks of practice and qualifying—each with their own distinct brand of drama—and climaxing in the grand finale on Memorial Day. This year, Act I boiled down to a high-speed poker game between Mario Andretti and Rick Mears. The two spent the first week of practice trading 220 + MPH laps, edging up to and surpassing 221 MPH to finish the week with identical 221.456s on Friday.

But the anticipated qualifying showdown ended before it began. Mario was caught-out in some residual oil-dry from Tom Bigelow's morning practice accident, savaging his right front tire, and had to hang it all out to reach 215 MPH. After Al Unser and Danny Sullivan recorded 215.270 and 216.214 respectively, Mears set the fastest qualifying run in Speedway history at 219.198 making it PC-17s One-Two-Three.

Week Two starts slowly and builds to a desperate tension by Sunday. Where time seemed limitless early in the month, the days fly past for those not yet "in the show." The big names waiting for the second week of qualifying—Foyt, Raul Boesel, Pancho Carter—were joined in waiting by highly touted rookies John Jones, Bill Vukovich III and John Andretti. In the end, Foyt, Boesel, Vuky and Andretti made it, although they were outshown by unheralded rookie Dominic Dobson whose 210.096 MPH made him the fastest rookie in history.

Act III, of course, is the largest single-day sporting event in the world. This race, however, was marred by a record number of caution periods beginning on the first lap when Brayton spun his Amway/Hemelgarn Lola, taking Guerrero and Tony Bettenhausen with him into the wall. After the clean-up, Sullivan bolted away from oval-meister Mears to an early lead, stretching his advantage through the first half of the race as Rick fell back with handling problems.

Sullivan's epic drive came to an abrupt halt against the Turn One wall on Lap 101 when the front wing adjuster worked loose and turned the sweet-handling PC-17 into an uncontrollable beast. That left Unser and Mears trading the lead.

Big Al would lose a lap to Mears during one of the 14 caution periods and Emerson Fittipaldi, driving with cool precision, moved into second. The day's final caution insured that Mears took his third Indy win under yellow while the Brazilian claimed second place.

The Indy car regulars reconvened a week later at the Milwaukee mile for the start of CART's "second season." Although Michael put the Kraco March 88C Cosworth on the pole, he faded in the race as Mario, Al Jr. and, finally, Mears led followed across the line by Sullivan.

Al Unser, Jr. matched Sullivan's four wins, but was still a bridesmaid. Photo/Bob Brodbeck.

Pieces of the Raynor Garage Door Lola flew when Derek Daly slammed the wall in Turn Three at Michigan. Daly's highest finish for the year was a fourth at Pocono. He was ninth in points. Photo/Bob Brodbeck.

Derrick Walker's (r.) move to the Porsche team from the Penske operation was tragically timely. His agreement with Al Holbert was cemented just days before Al was killed in a plane crash. Gary Grossenbacher (l.) was Holbert's right-hand man in the pits. Photo/Frank Ruch.

Sullivan's chief mechanic, Chuck Sprague, prepares for a pit stop. Sprague will replace Derrick Walker as team manager for the Penske team in '89. Photo/David Lubman.

The fact that Sullivan scorched to his sixth pole at Road America was less significant than the fact that the Penskes were getting poor fuel mileage. He barely coaxed his car into the pits for his second fuel stop, allowing Emmo to take the lead 'til the end. Sullivan was fourth. Photo/Rich Chenet.

Two fourths were Raul Boesel's best results for the season. Photo/Bob Brodbeck.

Although Milwaukee thrust Mears into the points lead, it also marked the start of a remarkable comeback. After leaving Indy lying 23rd in the standings, Sullivan would record five straight top-four finishes to assume the title lead at Michigan.

Having finished second at Milwaukee, a win was next on Sullivan's agenda. He accomplished just that on Portland's scenic 1.9-mile road course with a 17-second victory over Luyendyk. After beating Arie Luyendyk and Mears to the pole, Danny took an early race-day lead which he sacrificed to Arie, executing a half-spin in traffic. At the final pit stop, the Penske crew put Sullivan back in front where he stayed, followed home by Luyendyk in a car with a cracked exhaust header and without third gear.

Raul Boesel replaced Al Unser, Jr. in Doug Shierson's Domino's Pizza Cosworth Lola in '88. He was eighth for the year. Photo/Ron McQueeney.

From the grass confines of Portland, the CART teams next visited the concrete expanses of Cleveland's Burke Lakefront Airport on the Fourth of July weekend. There the Chevy boys had a new thorn in their side in the form of Bobby Rahal and the Judd-powered TrueSports Lola. Although Sullivan whisked to a stunning pole, beating Mears by a full second, at the checkered he had to settle for third behind Mario and Bobby.

Next came Toronto's wonderful street circuit where Sullivan claimed his third consecutive pole despite missing most of Saturday's qualifying session with electrical problems. Once again, though, the Penske PC-17 proved considerably less dominating in the turbulent air of raceday while Al Jr. and the Galles team got their race set-up perfect. While Danny grabbed the lead at the green, Unser zipped into the lead as Sullivan was inadvertently blocked by Foyt. When Danny was assessed a stop-and-go penalty for a pit lane violation after his second stop, the race was securely Unser's.

Luyendyk, here with car owner Dick Simon, had his most rewarding run at Portland. He started from the outside pole and finished second. Photo/Bob Brodbeck.

Arie Luyendyk might have won a race or two with a little luck in Dick Simon's Provimi-backed Lola, but crashes like this one at Pocono put him out more than once. Photo/Steve Swope.

Belgian Didier Theys joined the Dick Simon team at Portland, then ran mid-pack at selected races until Tamiami, where he outlasted more than half the field to place third behind Al Jr. and Rick Mears. Photo/Rich Chenet.

Kraco's team manager Barry Greene has a chat with Michael Andretti. The younger Andretti will join dad Mario in a second Chevy-powered Newman-Haas Lola in '89. Photo/Jim Hatfield.

Unser's hot streak continued the following weekend at the revised Meadowlands parking lot circuit, although he would be the first to admit there was a little luck involved this time—to say nothing of controversy. As befitting the Marlboro Grand Prix, Emerson Fittipaldi grabbed the pole in his Marlboro-sponsored car, the Patrick team having abandoned the troublesome March 88C in favor of a Lola T87/00 acquired from Newman/Haas Racing at Indianapolis. Emerson duly took the lead and, in fact, looked uncatchable until a full course yellow bunched the field. Moments after the restart, he made a slight bobble setting up for the fiendishly tight chicane and Al Jr. was alongside in a flash. "Emmo" refused to yield, the two bumped and the Brazilian plunged into the wall. Unser now had Mario to contend with as the result of the caution to remove the stricken Marlboro Lola from the track. After outbraking Al's Valvoline March to take the lead, Mario then had his K-Mart/Amoco Lola slow to a crawl on the final lap with a broken differential, enabling Unser to post his third win of 1988.

Although outpointed by his teammate since Milwaukee, Rick Mears had stayed in the title hunt with three top-six finishes. Still, the Michigan and Pocono 500s held the key to his championship hopes. He began with a pole at MIS, beating Al Unser and Mario Andretti at the last minute. Rick and Mario led early, with Big Al very much in the picture. But this would be a hard day on equipment as Mario and Mears spent time in the pits effecting repairs. Thus Sullivan took over after Unser nearly spun on water in the pit lane and, when Al fell by the wayside with engine problems, Danny was left to lead Rahal—who had, himself, led for some 20 laps at mid-race—home and bring Roger Penske his first win in the Michigan 500.

Long the leader in Indy car racing, the Cosworth engine took only one pole and never won a race. Photo/Steve Swope.

The Ilmor-Chevy's co-developer, Mario Illien, formerly of Cosworth. Photo/Art Flores.

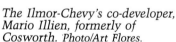

The dominant force of 1988 was the Ilmor-Chevrolet engine. All told, the Chevy won 14 of 15 poles, 14 of 15 races and led an astounding 1,911 of the year's 2,112 laps. Photo/Art Flores.

Mears rebounded at Pocono with his fourth pole of '88, becoming the first man in CART history to start first in all three 500-milers in the same year. Although Rick stormed to an early lead in his Penske entry, he was eliminated when he struck some debris from a wrecked car. But Big Al's flying PC-17 looked more than ready to take Unser-the-Older to the ninth 500 mile win of his illustrious career. Although Bobby Rahal kept Unser honest—even taking the lead by dint of determined driving and timely yellow flags—Al Sr. caught and passed the Budweiser Lola with contemptuous ease. But with 28 laps remaining, the Detroit Diesel-backed PC-17 was sidelined by a sick engine, leaving Rahal to take the maiden win for John Judd's V8.

Rahal's Pocono triumph propelled him to an improbable lead in the points race and, with TrueSports' "home track" looming next, Bobby was very much in the running for a third straight national title. But virtually nothing followed to form at Mid-Ohio. First came the stunning announcement that Rahal would be leaving TrueSports to accept a ride with Kraco Racing in 1989. Then came rain on Saturday that locked in Friday's provisional grid spots. A shower before the race meant a wet-tire start on a drying track. Although Mario jumped past Sullivan to take the early lead, Fittipaldi roared into first as the track dried, then pulled clear after switching to slicks on the first pit stop. Although Mario again gained the lead after the final pit stop, Emerson was not to be denied and hurtled back to the front once the racing resumed. He stalked Mario for several laps, before executing a breathtaking outside pass in Turn Eight and motoring away to the win. (Rahal was unceremoniously punted into the guardrail by a spinning Ludwig Heimrath, Jr., thus ending a perfectly dismal outing.)

The new alliance between Porsche and March and the hiring of Derrick Walker and aerodynamic wizard Tony Cicale should bring improved performance to the struggling Quaker State Porsche effort in 1989. Photo/Jim Hatfield.

Bobby Rahal scored the maiden win for John Judd's Honda V8 engine at Pocono, the only non-Chevy victory in '88. Photo/Art Flores.

From Sao Paulo, Brazil, Emerson Fittipaldi. "Emmo" set a qualifying record at the Meadowlands and a race lap record at Road America, placing seventh in the championship chase. Photo/David Taylor.

Fittipaldi proved he was the man to beat on the road courses and in the rain by taking two wins, first at a rainy Mid-Ohio, then at Road America. Photo/Art Flores.

From the twists and turns of Mid-Ohio it was on to Road America whose hills, long straights and tight corners combine to place a premium on fuel economy. Thus the fact that Sullivan scorched to his sixth pole of the year was less significant than the fact that the Penskes were getting poor fuel mileage. Sullivan duly led until the first pit stop when Fittipaldi emerged in first (Danny having been balked in pit lane by Foyt). Although Fittipaldi and Sullivan showed a clean pair of heels to the field, Danny just did manage to coax his car into the pits for his second fuel stop, leaving Fittipaldi all alone in first. Emerson held off Rahal for his second straight win as Mario trailed home third and Sullivan, for all his difficulties, took a crucial fourth.

The racers next journeyed to the tricky mile oval at Nazareth, Pennsylvania where, in a reversal of form, Sullivan took the pole and Mears took second. The race began with Danny moving over for Rick (a decision the two made in advance so that Mears wouldn't be jumped at the start), and unreeled at a dizzying rate. More than 120 laps sailed by at 160 + MPH before the day's lone caution appeared. By that point, the title hopes of Rahal, Unser and Fittipaldi had been crippled, the former two by a series of blistered tires (a problem that plagued much of the field) and the latter by a blown engine.

From the oval confines of Nazareth it was on to Laguna Seca near Monterey, California, the scenic 1.9-mile track now expanded to 2.2 miles by a slowish infield loop bypassing the testing—but dangerously fast—Turns One, Two and Three. Although the title hopes of Mario and Emerson were still mathematically alive, only Rahal and Al Unser, Jr. had a realistic hope of catching Sullivan and each desperately needed a win.

Sullivan had other plans, of course, and almost effortlessly claimed his eighth pole. At the start, Danny disappeared into the distance and was aided in his magic act when Fabi, who was several laps down after a couple of early spins, refused to yield to the pursuing Rahal, Mario and Al Jr. Rahal later ran short of brakes, then Unser smacked a kamikaze rabbit and was forced to pit, all of which promoted the Andrettis into second and third. There they remained with Michael outdistancing his father. Sullivan went on to his fourth win of the season and the first championship of his career.

From Laguna it was on to tropical Miami for the season finale. Final-ees, really, for the rainy Marlboro Challenge preceded the main race. The field went at it tooth and nail, but Michael came home the victor in his next-to-last start with Kraco, having announced a few days earlier that he would be joining Mario in a two car, K-Mart-sponsored Newman/Haas effort in 1989.

It's thumbs up for the Indy car racers at Laguna Seca. Photo/Taylors Photography.

Ed Pimm ran only two road races in the Orange Crush March 87C. Photo/Ron McQueeney.

Competing in only three races, Rich Vogler's best was an 11th at Pocono. Photo/Ken Brown-Competition Photographers.

Somebody has to do it. A Hemelgarn Racing crew member checks tire pressures. Photo/Tyler Photo Illustrators.

Teo Fabi rounded out the top 10 in points. Photo/Ron McQueeney.

Italy's Teo Fabi takes the bumps at Laguna Seca. At Nazareth he led briefly and brought the Quaker State Porsche home to fourth, a bittersweet result as the team's founder, Al Holbert, died the following weekend in a plane crash. Photo/Rich Chenet.

Defending CART titlist Bobby Rahal leads the pack at Road America. Rahal only won once but was always in the running for the championship. He placed third behind Sullivan and Unser, Jr. in points. Bobby's 13 finishes of 15 races underscored the reliability of the Judd-engined TrueSports Lola if not the speed. For 1989, Rahal will move over to the Kraco team and an ambitious Cosworth development program. Photos/Michael H. Dunn, Rich Chenet (inset).

The main race the next day started with a crunch as Boesel, Fabi and Fittipaldi tried to fit three cars into the single file Turn One with predictable results, taking Daly, Foyt, Guerrero, and Scott Brayton with them into instant retirement.

The restart saw Sullivan hammer away into the distance from his fifth straight pole, only to pit early with handling troubles. With multiple mechanical retirements, the final race of the year ultimately unwound in processional fashion with Al Unser, Jr. matching Sullivan's victory total at four while Mears, Didier Theys and Cogan followed him home.

Although Penske Racing won the championship, TrueSports and Galles Racing can look back on jobs well done. While Rahal rarely had the horses to match the bow-tie set, he kept his Judd-powered Lola in contention all year and, at Pocono, scored the only "un-Chevy" win of the season. Unser, Jr., on the other hand, had Chevy power but was handicapped by the problematic March 88C. Yet through some very determined driving and excellent work by the Galles team, he matched Sullivan win for win and came home second in points.

Mears, of course, might have won his fourth CART title but for some miserable mid-season luck, while Mario Andretti and the Newman/Haas team never quite regained their brilliant form of 1987. Like the rest of the Ford-Cosworth runners, Michael Andretti had to cope with a lack of power most of the year. Although he never gave less than 110 percent, it was clear that his relationship with the Kraco team had simply run its course and both parties can hope for better times in 1989. Patrick Racing, like Newman/Haas, finished less than half of the 15 races. Even the likes of Emerson Fittipaldi and Mario Andretti can't overcome that kind of handicap in so competitive a series as this.

Michael Andretti ended the season in sixth place. Photo/Tom Riles.

Another First Family member, John Andretti. Photo/Bob Brodbeck.

No, it's not a Yugo. It's Tony Bettenhausen's Lola backed by the Yugoslavian car company. A fourth at Michigan was the closest he came to a win. Photo/Ron McQueeney.

Longtime Lola
distributor and co-
owner of the
Newman-Haas team,
Carl Haas.
Photo/Tom Bernhardt.

CART's Rookie of the Year,
John Jones. Photo/Bob Brodbeck.

Roberto Guerrero took a
second at Phoenix.
Photo/Bob Brodbeck.

A.J. Foyt was named Most
Improved Driver. Photo/
Randy McKee.

A third at Indy was all Al
Unser, Sr. could accomplish.
Photo/Bob Brodbeck.

Al Unser, Sr. sat in for Roberto Guerrero in Vince Granatelli's STP Lola at Toronto, finishing ninth—three laps down. On the grid, Al Jr. gave dad some advice. Photo/Frank Ruch.

Rick Mears, with expert help from the capable Penske pit crew, took his third Indy 500 victory. Photos/David Taylor, Bruce R. Schulman (inset).

Rick Mears became the first man in CART history to start first in all three 500-mile races in a single year. The Indy 500 boiled down to a high-speed poker game between Mario Andretti and Rick Mears for the pole, with Mears winning the hand, both in qualifying and on race day. Photo/David Taylor.

The all-Penske front row at Indy: Mears, Sullivan, Unser, Sr. Photo/Jim Hatfield.

Raul Boesel and Team Shierson outdistanced the other non-winners (save for Michael Andretti) by a country mile but, strangely, never once mounted the victory podium. Similarly, Derek Daly and Raynor Racing never finished higher than fourth and were further handicapped by appalling fortune through the first half of the season. Rookies of the Year, past and present, finished tied for 10th in points in the form of Teo Fabi and John Jones. Fabi and the Quaker State Porsche team paid their dues this season and look to better times in the near future. Jones developed steadily under the patient guidance of Frank Arciero's team, finishing the season on the verge of joining the front-runners.

Elsewhere, Dick Simon's star finally began to rise with the arrival of Arie Luyendyk and the Provimi sponsorship. Ably backed up by Didier Theys, Arie might have won a race or two with a little luck. The same, alas, cannot be said for either Hemelgarn or Granatelli Racing, both of which floundered in 1988 after coming to the verge of greatness the prior year.

Nineteen-eighty-nine shapes up as an intriguing season, if for no other reason than the schedule now includes the tower-shaded city streets of Detroit where CART has replaced the F1 circus.

In the season opener, at Phoenix, A. J. Foyt scored his best for the year, a fourth. Photo/Ron McQueeney.

Coming to the verge of greatness in '87, the Granatelli Racing team floundered in 1988. Roberto Guerrero and Vince Granatelli held a meeting. Photo/Bob Brodbeck.

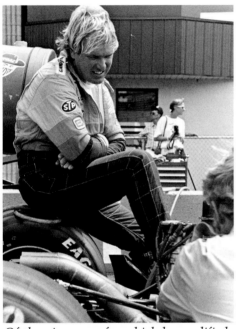

Of the nine races for which he qualified, Dale Coyne was running at the finish in only two, yet took home a whopping paycheck of $134,323. Photo/Bob Brodbeck.

Bobby Rahal will be replaced by Scott Pruett on the TrueSports team in '89. Photo/Stan Clinton.

Pre-race festivities often include parachutists landing on the front straight—before they grid the cars, of course. Photo/Ken Brown-Competition Photographers.

Pocono's front row: Mears, Sullivan, Rahal. Rahal won. Photo/Steve Swope.

The ultimate professional, Mario Andretti.
Photo/David Taylor.

Mario Andretti opened the year with a resounding victory at Phoenix, then followed it up with another at Cleveland, where he squeaked out the win over Rahal by the season's closest margin of less than a second! Photo/David Taylor.

Al Unser, Jr. leads Michael Andretti. These youngsters are a long way from being over the hill! Photo/David Taylor.

Team co-owner Paul Newman and crew cheered Mario's win at Cleveland. Photo/Ron McQueeney.

The engine war is also heating up to levels previously unknown in CART. The Chevys will be back, augmented by the second Newman/Haas Lola for Michael Andretti. Judd has formed a three-team development partnership, spearheaded by TrueSports and including the Shierson and Raynor teams.

Cosworth, too, has launched an ambitious development program for the Bobby Rahal-piloted Kraco car as well as Simon's two-car effort for Luyendyk and new recruit Scott Brayton. Meanwhile, don't forget the Quaker State Porsche team which will be back in 1989 with renewed determination, new team manager Derrick Walker (ex-Penske Racing), new aerodynamic wizard Tony Cicale (ex-Newman/Haas), and a new chassis built in cooperation with March.

Scott Pruett (#11) leads John Jones and Danny Sullivan onto the straight at Mid-Ohio. Pruett subbed for Kevin Cogan, injured at Toronto. Photo/Sidell Tilghman.

Derek Daly and Raynor Racing never finished higher than fourth and were further handicapped by appalling fortune through the first half of the season. Daly and chief mechanic Kim Green confer. Photo/Bob Brodbeck.

Rookie Scott Atchison (r.) gets some car-handling tips from Rick Mears. Photo/Bob Brodbeck.

Mario Andretti and Oscar winner Paul Newman at Indy. Unflappable team timers Kathy Beadle and Bernie Haas are oblivious to all but their work. Photo/Tom Riles.

In the closing laps at Pocono young John Andretti crashed heavily in pit lane. A bolt worked free in the rear suspension of the Skoal Bandit Lola. He escaped with minor injuries. Photo/Tom Bernhardt.

Al Holbert talks with Quaker State Porsche driver Teo Fabi. The sport lost a giant in American racing when Holbert was killed. *Photo/Sidell Tilghman.*

Huge crowds are a regular sight at Indy car races. Here, at Michigan they were treated to another great win by champion Danny Sullivan. *Photo/Michael H. Dunn.*

An on-again, off-again rainy Marlboro Challenge at Tamiami saw Michael Andretti score his only win of the season. Marlboro-backed Emerson Fittipaldi was second and Raul Boesel rounded out the top three. Al Unser, Jr. led most of the laps until he crunched the Turn Nine wall only one lap from the finish. *Photo/David Taylor.*

His '88 season couldn't match the drama of 1987, and Michael Andretti wound up sixth in points, just behind dad Mario. He came home the victor in his next-to-last start with Kraco, the Marlboro Challenge, after announcing he'd move over to Newman-Haas and a two-car team for him and Mario.
Photo/David Taylor.

WoO/Copenhagen-Skoal Shootout

by JOE SCALZO,
CIRCLE TRACK

***T**HE NERVE-WRACKED,* chain-smoking Ted Johnson seems to sustain and stimulate himself on a steady diet of nicotine and Dr. Pepper. Yet for the hyperactive 54-year-old founder and president of the World of Outlaws (WoO) sanctioning body, and its Copenhagen-Skoal national championship series, 1988 must have seemed like a trial, a sentence, a punishment for Johnson-wasn't-sure-what.

Hostilities erupted early, then rapidly grew worse. They actually began in February in Florida where WoO drivers ushered in the new year by flipping one another out of Tampa's State Fair Speedway; and they continued in Arizona when a couple of race teams had a violent uprooting of personnel.

But during the following week, at the awards banquet in Long Beach, California, where the 1987 cash awards were distributed, a car owner, accepting his prizes, unexpectedly boke down in the middle of his thank-you speech and started crying; the audience saluted his tears by cutting in with warm, emotional applause; and, briefly, the WoO became one big happy family again. Very briefly. Shortly after this expression of sentimentality, the same weeping car owner had a quick, but devastating, difference of opinion with a rival driver and appeared at the weekend's Ascot Park races bearing a knot on his forehead (The strife seemed contagious. The dance band at the WoO fete had problems of its own: Its lead female singer experienced sudden kidney pains while performing and had to be hospitalized; and her hastily recruited replacement, the band's pregnant back-up singer, subsequently went into false labor during her fill-in performance.).

Greg Wooley (#23) makes a vain attempt to hold off Steve Kinser at Eagle Raceway. Kinser won the big ones 27 times in 1988, the third time in the World of Outlaws' 11-year history that he's won more than 25 features. Photo/Bob Mays.

Though only occasionally demonstrating the crushing authority he possessed last season, in 1988 Steve Kinser captured his ninth Copenhagen-Skoal national championship. Teamwork was vital. Photo/Mike Arthur.

Departing California without further pain, Johnson and his outlaws arrived in Texas for the next round of races. Something else happened. Johnson did not yet know it, but a cabal of his WoO owners were talking revolt. Following a hysterical mass meeting in a crowded Dallas motel room, conducted in an atmosphere, "reminiscent of a lynch mob," according to one of them, the revolutionaries, abruptly tired of a decade's worth of Johnson's leadership, vowed to boycott future WoO races. The boycott never materialized, partly because Johnson, in a flattering, conciliatory gesture, got the would-be lynchers to call off their coup by hastily naming six of them to something he called the Car Owners Advisory Board.

Suddenly sapped by all the fighting, and by now thoroughly fed up with and suspicious of one another, everybody summoned up what remained of their energies to complete the remaining seven-months-worth of nighttime WoO dirt races. But no sooner had the dreary season ended in October when fresh horror arose to confront Ted Johnson. A brand new sprint car club, the United Sprint Association (USA), administered by Johnson's own former directors of competition, marketing and public relations, appeared to blandly announce it intended to pirate away all of Johnson's WoO drivers, car owners, sponsors and race dates.

It's three wide at I-55 Speedway, as Jac Haudenschild (#18), Sammy Swindell (#1) and Doug Wolfgang line up for the flag. Photo/Todd Hunter.

Sammy Swindell, second in the standings, was the only driver to earn the Autolite Pacesetter Award for fastest time, win the Fram Dash and take the feature all in the same one-night event. Photo/Taylors Photography.

One car's tires for a night. Photo/Krieger Photography.

Sheila Bouvin, the lady with the wildest paint job in sprint car racing.
Photo/Jim Phillipson.

The richest short-track racing series in history boasted a $4 million purse, handing out more than $100,000 to six drivers in 1988. The top 10 averaged $172,870 in prize money, up almost $35,000 from '87. Photo/Jim Phillipson.

Steve Kinser may have captured his ninth title, but he didn't dominate in '88. Photo/Randy McKee.

And the race is on. Photo/Jim Phillipson.

WoO competition doesn't always bring out the best in the locals. Here, at Baylands Raceway, Marco Bowers (#14B) nudges Joe Donahoo out of the way. Photo/Jim Phillipson.

Lealand McSpadden does a wheelie at Ascot. Photo/Mike Arthur.

Nat Polen demonstrates the wing's second most important job. Photo/Jim Phillipson.

Andy Hillenburg was the best of the rookies, finishing his first full WoO season in sixth. Photo/Krieger Photography.

Immediately jumping aboard the USA bandwagon as supporters came Johnson's two big stars—perhaps his only stars—Steve Kinser and Sammy Swindell. Seeming also ready to jump, was Johnson's new Car Owners Advisory Board, the majority of whose members promptly entered their vehicles and drivers in an October-November swing of USA races in Arizona, Tennessee and Texas.

If you are wondering what all this fighting, feuding, plotting, and maneuvering had to do with improving the quality of sprint car racing in 1988, the answer is, "very little." Thus, 1988 was a sour year. It wasn't even a competitive year. Though only occasionally demonstrating the crushing authority he possessed last season, Steve Kinser did capture his ninth Copenhagen-Skoal national championship. He also won 27 races (including his third consecutive Knoxville Nationals), three times more than Swindell, the series' frustrated runner-up. Kinser did have one bad moment early in the year at Manzanita Speedway in Phoenix, Arizona, when he inhaled too many methane fumes and had to visit a hospital where, for some reason, he was given a flu shot.

Runner-up Sammy Swindell won eight features and eight preliminary events. Photo/Krieger Photography.

Fourth in points, Dave Blaney. Photo/Krieger Photography.

Winner of six features, Doug Wolfgang. Photo/Kriger Photography.

Steve Kinser's cousin Mark led the Shootout standings through three events, then fell back to fifth by the end of the season. He married Cindy Moore on December 3. Photo/Phil Dullinger.

This seemed to actually give him the flu and put him temporarily off his form.

As if to underscore the sort of abominable year it really was, there were also the crippling injuries to WoO's most popular, most unlucky driver, Brad Doty. He received them not in a WoO race but in Ohio, at Eldora Speedway, trying to win an unsanctioned meet with a $50,000 first place purse. His friends and admirers sympathetically tallied the circumstances contributing to the disaster: First, there was Doty's mistaken decision, regarded as courageous at the time, to resume sprint racing after nearly losing an eye in a 1986 melee at Williams Grove, Pennsylvania; then there was the ironic, lethal fact that one of the crucial cars involved in his multi-car spill was his own former ride, which he'd just recently quit; and lastly, there was the amazing fact that the wreck took place at Eldora, almost Doty's home track. All these things, plus Doty's wife being pregnant with the couple's third child at the time of the accident, made what happened to Doty seem outrageous and almost unbearable.

Just like — as Ted Johnson might agree — 1988 itself, often seemed.

In tenth, Danny Smith. Photo/Krieger Photography.

An intense Bobby Allen was 12th for the year. Photo/Krieger Photography.

Jac Haudenschild. Photo/Al Steinberg.

Jac Haudenschild (#1T) and Tim Green take it side by side at Baylands. Jac earned his third consecutive top-10 ranking, driving four different cars. Photo/Jim Phillipson.

USAC/Sprint Cars

by JOE SCALZO
SENIOR EDITOR, *CIRCLE TRACK*

*T*WO PERSONALITIES COMPLETELY consumed the U.S. Auto Club's national sprint car series in 1988. One was Steve Butler, who dominated with his driving and by earning his third consecutive USAC seasonal title. The second was Gary Sokola, who had previously been the long-time ruler of the California Racing Association until, late in 1987, he was pirated away from the CRA by USAC to become the new supervisor of USAC's chronically weak sprint division.

Sokola's pirating-away had historic overtones. Almost ten years earlier, in a nearly identical situation, USAC had stripped the CRA of its then-President, and Sokola's predecessor, Don Peabody. Exactly like Sokola today, Peabody in 1978 had been instructed to shake up and rehabilitate the poor sprint car division, which even in the Seventies was already ill; and during the opening months of his reign, Peabody appeared to be doing just

that. Then he became one of the seven officials to be lost in the notorious USAC plane crash of that April, and in the years since it often had seemed as if the future of USAC sprint car racing had been lost with Peabody.

Precisely like Peabody a decade before him, Sokola harvested some 1988 successes. In 1986, USAC had sanctioned a paltry 11 races. Sokola more than doubled that number and got as many as 40 cars to come to some of them. He helped restore pavement racing to USAC's previously all-dirt agenda. Because he was a product of the CRA's wing-free environment, he had been expected to try and indoctrinate USAC with his anti-wing views. Instead, proving himself an unpredictable ruler, Sokola turned an about-face and caused ripples of surprise with early rulings seeming to favor the over-the-cockpit lids. The future of USAC sprint car racing now exhibits a renewed surge of interest.

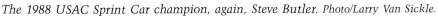

The 1988 USAC Sprint Car champion, again, Steve Butler. Photo/Larry Van Sickle.

Winning only once in '88, Steve Butler went wingless at Salem Speedway. Photo/Larry Van Sickle.

Steve Butler became the first man to ever win the USAC Sprint Car championship three years in a row. Photo/Larry Van Sickle.

Jim Childers brought his pavement Sprinter from Florida to run with USAC at Salem. Photo/Larry Van Sickle.

Jack Hewitt nearly flipped during qualifying at Lawrenceburg Speedway, but it didn't prevent him from winning the feature from the back of the pack. Hewitt landed in third in the standings. Photo/John Mahoney.

CRA/Sprint Cars

by JOE SCALZO
SENIOR EDITOR, *CIRCLE TRACK*

Ron Shuman received the winner's wreath the first night CRA raced in 1988 at Manzanita Speedway in Phoenix, and never relinquished the points lead. He replaced Brad Noffsinger as the 1988 CRA champion. Photo/Phil Dullinger.

BETTER THAN A DECADE'S worth of hard living on the road at last convinced the protean openwheel driver Ron Shuman to halt his traveling and look for a regular racing home. He found one at Ascot Park in Los Angeles with the wingless Sprint cars of the California Racing Association. He won 14 main events, including the big Don Peabody Memorial 50-lapper on a muddy track and replaced Brad Noffsinger, a NASCAR Winston Cup defector, as CRA champion.

Running wingless, Ron Shuman won 14 main events at Ascot Park, including the big Don Peabody Memorial 50-lapper on a muddy track. Photo/Mike Arthur.

USAC/Silver Crown

Silver Crown sprinters (below center) take off at the Illinois State Fairgrounds. Indy 500 veteran Steve Chassey sped from 20th starting spot to claim the Tony Bettenhausen 100 win. Photo/Dr. H.C. Hunter.

Steve Butler was crowned the 1988 USAC/Valvoline Silver Crown Champion for the first time, without winning a single race! Photo/Larry Van Sickle.

Only Jack Hewitt's Eldora Speedway victory kept all nine different races from having different winners. Hewitt ended up second in points. Photo/John Mahoney.

Victorious at the Wisconsin State Fairgrounds, George Snider was third in the final standings, behind Vogler and Hewitt. Photo/John Mahoney.

Chuck Gurney won one, at the Indiana State Fairgrounds, in his Genessee "Beer Wagon." Photo/John Mahoney.

Scoring 16 feature victories, just one less than Mel Kenyon's all-time USAC record of 17 set over 20 years ago, Rich Vogler grabbed his fifth USAC/Jolly Rancher Candies Midget series championship in 1988. Photo/Larry Van Sickle.

"Hollywood" Sleepy Tripp (below left) became the 1988 USAC West Coast champion in Midgets. Photo/Mike Arthur.

He scored no wins, but Terry Wente still placed second to Vogler in national USAC Midget points. Photo/ Larry Van Sickle.

Driving the Miller Special, Vogler boosted his career total to 90 Midget wins. Photo/Larry Van Sickle.

Chuck Gurney set fast time during trials for the Hut Hundred, but flipped on the first lap, emerging unhurt. He won once, at the penultimate season event at Ascot, but didn't make it into the top 10 at year's end. Photo/John Mahoney.

Tragedy struck the midget ranks when Jeri Rice, one of the few women to run a USAC Midget, was killed while viewing a race in New Mexico. Photo/Mike Arthur.

Gordy Ward survived this flip with only a few fractures and burns at the Hut Hundred. Jack Hewitt slid to the outside. Photo/John Mahoney.

IMSA/Camel GTP

by **BILL LOVELL**
SENIOR CONTRIBUTING EDITOR, *AUTOWEEK*

*I*T WAS A CRISP EARLY SPRING Sunday in the rolling red hills of north Georgia, a proper time for beginnings. Even though IMSA's long season was already well underway, with the 24 Hours of Daytona, the Grand Prix of Miami and the 12 Hours of Sebring already in the record books, it was time for one team to come to the point and take charge.

There were candidates aplenty. Jaguar, with major support from Castrol and Dunlop, had arrived with a new team led by England's Tom Walkinshaw and Indy car veterans Tony Dowe and Ian Reed. And they'd arrived in splendid fashion, winning the 24 Hours of Daytona, Porsche's private party for the previous 11 years. Jaguar had the car—the stunning new XJR-9 penned by Tony Southgate; the drivers (Martin Brundle, John Nielsen and Raul Boesel shared the winning car; Brundle and Nielsen would essentially do the whole season, joined by Jan Lammers and Davy Jones); and, just as importantly, the budget, the exact sum of which was undisclosed but reliably rumored to be enough to win a Republican a seat in the Politburo.

After Daytona, many were ready to concede the season to Team Castrol Jaguar, including Bob Wollek, whose Porsche completed the 24 Hours in second, a lap down from the winner. "I can see Porsche winning maybe two or three races all year," he said, "and Jaguar all the rest."

No one can accuse Wollek of not putting his money where his mouth is: While still driving for Porsche the Frenchman opened a Jaguar dealership in his native Strasbourg. Besides which, he was half-right.

Two of those Porsche wins came in quick order. In Miami, Price Cobb and James Weaver in Rob Dyson's Blaupunkt Porsche avoided a hideous foul up at pit exit that cost several contenders critical time and took the lead. Cobb then held off a furious charge by Nielsen in the Jaguar to win by just four-thousandths-of-a-second, the second-closest finish in IMSA history. In contrast, Klaus Ludwig and Hans Stuck cruised to victory at Sebring with the largest margin of victory in 20 years, their Bruce Leven-owned Havoline Porsche crossing the line over nine laps ahead of the Joest Porsche of Winter/Jelinski/Barilla.

Geoff Brabham, the 1988 IMSA Camel GTP champion, discusses Nissan's winning strategy with crew members. Photo/Sidell Tilghman.

Kas Kastner, Nissan Motor Corp.'s racing manager, knew the best tricks in the book to mastermind Nissan's Camel GT dominance in '88. *Photo/Sidell Tilghman.*

Australian Geoff Brabham took the Nissan GTP ZX-T to an unprecedented eight victories in a row, but Porsche won the manufacturers title. *Photo/Sidell Tilghman.*

The new Castrol Jaguar team of Martin Brundle, Raul Boesel and John Nielsen won the hard-fought Daytona 24-hour race as expected, but the rest of the season was a losing battle. Photo/Stan Clinton.

Tom Gloy was in the hot seat when the engine blew on his Tom Milner Racing Ford GTP in practice for the Daytona 24 Hours. Photo/Tom Bernhardt.

The "39 Hours of Florida," IMSA's traditional Grapefruit League, was history. Now, at Road Atlanta, the real Camel GT season was about to begin. It began with yet another new winner, the fast but (heretofore) fragile Electramotive Engineering Nissan GTP ZX-T fielded by Don Devendorf. Driven by Geoff Brabham and John Morton, the win didn't come easily: The Nissan had to make one more fuel stop than the second-place Nielsen/John Watson Jaguar and suffered a brief fire in the pits. But in the late going Brabham made up a 33-second deficit in 25 laps and just blew past Nielsen on the backstraight to win by not quite four seconds.

We, of course, couldn't know it then, but we'd just witnessed the story of the whole season. For the next seven races, the only variables would be which driver shared the victory stand with Brabham and which team would finish second. Starting with Road Atlanta, Brabham and the Nissan won an incredible eight races in a row, shattering the old IMSA consecutive victories record of five. At West Palm Beach, Lime Rock, Mid-Ohio, Watkins Glen, Elkhart Lake, Portland and Sears Point, it was the same old story: The Nissan was all-world, and everyone else was running for best-in-class.

Jaguar's team manager, Tony Dowe, chats with Martin Brundle. Brundle was fifth in points for the year. Photo/Sidell Tilghman.

The start of the Daytona 24-hour race saw three Jaguars, seven Porsche 962s, one Pontiac GTP, one Ford GTP, a Cosworth Tiga and a Buick March. It marked the beginning of an exciting IMSA season. Photo/Geoffrey Hewitt.

*American-living-in-Rome
Eddie Cheever.
Photo/Geoffrey Hewitt.*

Co-drivers varied. John Morton was injured in a terrifying practice crash at Lime Rock, his brand-new car doing a back flip at the crest of the hill. Brabham drove solo to the win there, and was paired with Tom Gloy at Mid-Ohio. Morton came back to co-drive at the Glen and Road America, and Brabham soloed at Portland and Sears Point.

Four more times during the streak a Jaguar came second: Lammers and Jones once (West Palm Beach) and Brundle/Nielsen thrice (Lime Rock, Mid-Ohio and Sears Point). Last year's series champion, Chip Robinson, teamed with Derek Bell in the Holbert Porsche for runner-up honors at Watkins Glen and Road America, while Morton gave Nissan its only one-two finish with a fine second at Portland.

But the question all those guys—except, naturally, for Morton, who would leave late in the year for more rehabilitation and be replaced by Derek Daly—were asking, as each second place became more frustrating than the one before, was simple: What do they have that we don't have?

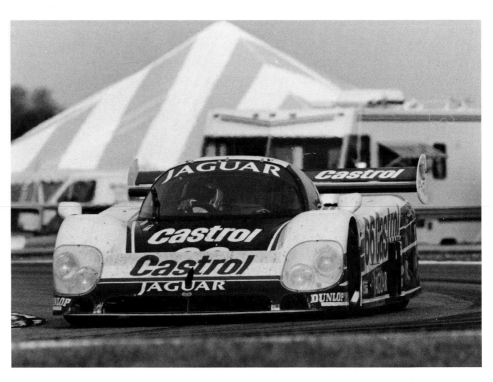

*The #66 Jaguar XJR-9 was driven to a third in the Daytona 24-hour race by Eddie Cheever and Englishmen Johnny Dumfries and John Watson.
Photo/Geoffrey Hewitt.*

Well, horsepower, for one thing, though the Nissan folks tried to downplay their advantage there. Handling, for another. For 1988 Nissan hauled out a new chassis designed by Trevor Harris. All that was left of the old Lola was its basic shape, and even that was extensively redone by Yoshi Suzuka. The result was a car Brabham said was, "two and a half times stiffer than last year's." In addition, the new car was a perfect match for Goodyear's new 17-inch radials, making the parting with last year's sponsor, Bridgestone, a divorce made in heaven.

Then the Nissan crew traded some of that horsepower for downforce, swapping a little top-end speed for a lot of stick. Finally, with old Triumph maestro Kas Kastner in charge of motorsports at Nissan, the team got sufficient support from the factory to run for the title — the drivers title, anyway.

Although Cobb and Weaver broke the streak with a win at San Antonio, Brabham came back to nail down the drivers championship—and his ninth win of the year—at Columbus. The manufacturers crown eluded the team when Brabham crashed at the season's finale at Del Mar and teammate Daly finished fourth behind the winning Lammers/Brundle Jaguar and the Porsches of Wollek and Ludwig. Porsche staggered away with the title, winning by a single point!

That's what the record books show. Anyone who followed this Camel GT season, though, knows that the year belonged to Brabham and the Nissan: lock and stock, if not quite barrel.

Price Cobb won two races, more than any other Porsche driver, except for teammate James Weaver who shared the victories, ending up third in points. Photo/Tom Bernhardt.

Porsche won the manufacturers championship by one point over Nissan at the last race, and it was the #16 Porsche 962 of Dyson Racing for Price Cobb and James Weaver that scored the most points towards this title. Photo/Stan Clinton.

Bob Wollek's 962 (#67) squeezes by the remains of Michael Andretti's 962 and Tom Gloy's Ford Probe during practice at Miami. Michael didn't start the race, Gloy ended up ninth. Photo/Stan Clinton.

For 1988 Nissan hauled out a new chassis, then the crew traded some horsepower for downforce, swapping a little top-end speed for a lot of stick, and with old Triumph maestro Kas Kastner in charge of motorsports at Nissan, the team got sufficient support from the factory to run for the title—the driver's title anyway. Geoff Brabham drove only 12 of the 14 races scheduled to win the championship handily. Photos/Sidell Tilghman (inset), Jim Hatfield.

Some cars have the owner's name painted on in bold letters. The Bayside Motorsports team chose to use the boss's likeness. Photo/Tom Bernhardt.

Old Prune Face

Germans Stuck and Ludwig won the Sebring 12-hour race in Bruce Leven's Havoline 962, nine laps ahead of the second-place car! Photo/Stan Clinton.

The real prune face, fun-loving Bruce Leven of Seattle. Photo/Tom Bernhardt.

Photographers and announcers ducked when Hans Stuck and Klaus Ludwig uncorked the champagne in Sebring's victory circle. Photo/Geoffrey Hewitt.

It was a race-long battle between the front-row starters at Watkins Glen. The Brabham/Morton Nissan won—again—and Chip Robinson and Derek Bell scored one of their few good finishes (second) in the Miller 962. Photo/Sidell Tilghman.

AN ELEGANT APPLICATION OF JAGUAR'S V-12 RACING EXPERIENCE.

THE 1989 JAGUAR XJ-S

When it comes to V-12 power, no one has more experience than Jaguar, on the track or on the road.

Today, Jaguar leads the world in V-12 production. In 1988, racing V-12 Jaguars won their second consecutive World Sports Car Championship and the world's two toughest 24-hour endurance races—Daytona and Le Mans.

Powered by the production version of Jaguar's race-proven, overhead cam V-12, the sleek and sensuous XJ-S performs in a manner befitting a true grand touring car. It offers the vivid response of 262 horsepower. Yet it moves with the silence and smoothness that only twelve cylinders can deliver.

Inside, the driver and passengers ride in quiet comfort and handcrafted Jaguar luxury. The 2 + 2 cabin is trimmed with lustrous burl walnut. Supple leather faces the front and rear seats, console and armrests. The new sports-contoured front seats incorporate power-variable lumbar support and tempera-ture-controlled heating elements.

For 1989, the S-type's impeccable road manners have been further refined. An advanced anti-lock (ABS) braking system now complements the power-assisted, four-wheel disc brakes. Wider, V speed-rated tires, mounted on new spoke-pattern alloy wheels, sharpen the sure-footed abilities of Jaguar's renowned four-wheel independent suspension.

The XJ-S also comes with the comforting assurance of Jaguar's extensive three-year/36,000-mile warranty and comprehensive Service-On-Site℠ Roadside Assistance Plan. Your dealer can provide details on this plan and on Jaguar's limited warranty, applicable in the USA and Canada. Test drive the most elegant application of Jaguar's V-12 experience. For the name of your nearest Jaguar dealer, call toll-free: 1-800-4-JAGUAR.

JAGUAR CARS INC., LEONIA, NJ 07605

ENJOY TOMORROW.
BUCKLE UP TODAY.

JAGUAR XJ-S

John Morton had a bad year. Photo/David Taylor.

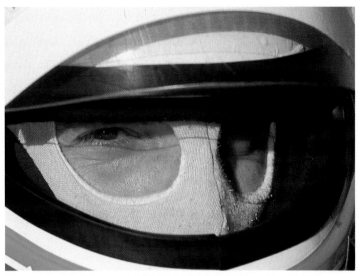

Monte Carlo's Mauro Baldi drove for BFG. Photo/David Taylor.

Sunset at Sebring as the Dyson Porsche aims for the first turn. Photo/Bob Fischer.

Two wheels up was standard fare at Lime Rock for most of the GTP cars. Morton took it one terrifying step further. Photo/Geoffrey Hewitt.

"It was an airborne fireball," someone said. John Morton's Nissan did a back-flip and burst into flames as it scaled Lime Rock's notorious uphill turn. Miraculously, Morton walked away, returning to the team several races later. But it was clear he was still hurting, and Kas Kastner called in Derek Daly to take over. Photos/Gene"Roz"Rosintoski.

Bob Earl was impressive in the Collins & Aikman Pontiac GTP, but engine reliability was a problem. Photo/Al Steinberg.

The Pontiac GTP had good qualifying speeds, but poor race performances. Pontiac announced mid-season it was backing out of IMSA for '89. Photo/Geoffrey Hewitt.

Chevy Fabcar drivers Chip Mead (l.) and Tim McAdam (r.) talk it over with Fabcar's Dave Klym. Photo/Randy McKee.

Dave Klym, known for his Porsche chassis fabrication, developed the Chevy Fabcar for GTP, but had limited success. Photo/Geoffrey Hewitt.

" The heights by great men reached and kept
Were not attained by sudden flight,
But they, while their companions slept,
Were toiling upward in the night."
The Ladder of Saint Augustine, Henry
Wadsworth Longfellow. *Photo/Bill Stahl.*

Two driving forces behind Nissan's success: team owner Don Devendorf and chassis designer Trevor Harris. Photo/Geoffrey Hewitt.

A. J. Foyt and the late Al Holbert. Foyt drove in early-season races. Photo/Geoffrey Hewitt.

Andial engines built by Alwin Springer for the Porsche 962s were still reliable, but no match for the Nissan's power. Photo/Werner Fritz.

Elliott Forbes-Robinson had a frustrating season in the Hendrick Corvette GTP. Photo/Jerry Crawford.

Rob Dyson sometimes co-drove with Bruce Leven in Bayside Motorsports' second 962. Photo/Werner Fritz.

West Germany's John Nielsen won only one race, but earned second place in points behind Brabham. Photo/Werner Fritz.

Sarel van der Merwe won his 11th rally championship in South Africa but no races for the Hendrick Corvette GTP team. Photo/Jerry Crawford.

Englishman James Weaver co-drove with Price Cobb to two wins, ending up fourth in the championship. Photo/Werner Fritz.

Jaguar driver Davy Jones was sixth in points, with two runner-up finishes his best for the season. Photo/Werner Fritz.

Chip Robinson (r.) couldn't repeat his championship-winning season of '87. When Al Holbert (l.) was killed in a plane crash, the team packed it in for the rest of the year, leaving Chip without a job. Photo/David Taylor.

Al Holbert's long association with Porsche is legendary. Al worked hard to make the Porsche a success in the U.S. He wouldn't see the 1988 manufacturers championship come down to the last race, where Porsche bested Nissan by one point. Photo/David Taylor.

Long-time Holbert Racing driver Derek Bell was also out of a ride. Photo/Jeff Carson.

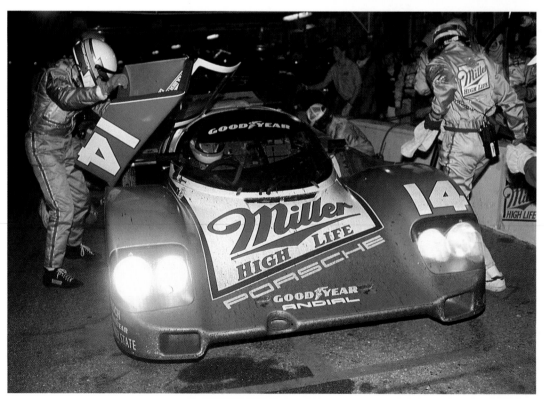

Decked out in new Miller Beer colors, the Holbert team hoped to win their second straight Daytona 24-hour race. They led the most laps but failed to take the checkered flag, ending up seventh. Photo/David Taylor.

Al Holbert's team took the Porsche 962 to 23 IMSA GTP wins before Al's death. Al remains the winningest professional road racer in the U.S. with 64 victories, 49 of them in Camel GT, making him IMSA's all-time winner. Photo/Bob Fischer.

Bruce Leven made few appearances with his Porsche 962, winning Sebring and taking a pair of seconds at Columbus and Del Mar. Klaus Ludwig was the main driver. Bruce drove the car solo and with Rob Dyson when Klaus wasn't around. Photo/Sidell Tilghman.

Two Corvette GTPs made up Rick Hendrick's IMSA stable, with top pilots Sarel van der Merwe and Elliott Forbes-Robinson driving, but their lackluster performance put an end to the team's effort at Del Mar until further notice. Photo/Geoffrey Hewitt.

Tom Milner bought the Ford Probes originally campaigned by Zakspeed, but the team's early-season performance was mediocre. Photo/Geoffrey Hewitt.

Peerless Racing showed up with their newly-designed Corvette GTP for David Hobbs and Jack Baldwin at Columbus. Their fourth place finish was impressive. Photo/Geoffrey Hewitt.

Geoff Brabham's teammate, John Morton, shared four of Brabham's victories. Morton drove a second Nissan solo at Portland to make it 1-2 for the team, and again at Sears Point, where he was eighth. He ended the season ninth in points. Photo/Sidell Tilghman.

The inaugural GTE World Challenge of Tampa saw a meager GTP and Group C field. Geoff Brabham, teamed with John Morton, blasted away from the competition, underscoring the Nissan team's dominance of the sport against all takers. Photo/Sidell Tilghman.

Nissan's strongest foe was the Torno Group C Porsche 962 of Oscar Larrauri and Massimo Sigala. Fuel restrictions on the Group C cars forced them to run slower. They settled for second, 34 seconds down. Photo/Sidell Tilghman.

Tom Milner's Dunlop-shod Ford Probes showed up in force. The #7 car, driven by Chip Robinson and Italy's Ruggero Melgrati, took a fourth, one lap down. The matching #6 car, driven by Pete Halsmer, was disqualified for an illegal restrictor plate. Photo/Sidell Tilghman.

To learn how to build a better car, we took a lot of demanding courses.

GTP ZX-Turbo at Lime Rock Park.

300 ZX at Road Atlanta.

300 ZX-Turbo at Laguna Seca.

GTP ZX-Turbo at Mid Ohio Sports Car Course.

300 ZX-Turbo at Road America.

The toughest race of all.

For years, racing and winning have been important priorities at Nissan®

We've competed in thousands of races. Taken 58 SCCA National Championships. Set an IMSA GTP record* with eight wins in a row. And sponsored drivers, racing teams and events all across the country. In all classes and types of racing.

But racing means more to us than just a nice trophy collection. What we find out on the racetrack helps us improve the other cars we build. Cars that have to handle even tougher situations.

*Single driver, single team, single season.

Like rush hour traffic. Or slippery school crossings.

And for as long as we continue learning, we'll definitely continue racing.

Because no matter how much you already know, we think you can never take enough classes.

Built for the Human Race.™

96

IMSA/Camel Lights

by BILL LOVELL
SENIOR CONTRIBUTING EDITOR, *AUTOWEEK*

ONE YEAR AGO, TOM HESSERT was just another face in the crowd, and rather deep in the crowd at that. This year he's IMSA's Camel Lights Champion. The way he did it is simple, if a trifle expensive. All he did was conduct his Lights campaign as if he were running GTP.

Camel Lights isn't exactly IMSA's glamour division. The prize money isn't much, and running as a race-within-a-race, the smaller prototypes get only a small fraction of the public attention enjoyed by their bigger and faster brothers. So the usual driver line-up on a Lights team tends to consist of a car owner/driver and a series of guys who rent seat time on a per-race or season basis. This helps pay the bills, but isn't likely to produce a consistent front runner.

That pretty much describes Hessert's program in 1987. But after the season, Hessert asked the late Al Holbert—IMSA's all-time winningest driver—for a little advice. Holbert being Holbert, he gave it to him straight. "Maybe," he said, "you ought to pay somebody to co-drive the car."

Tom Hessert (c.) put an end to Jim Downing's three-year reign to become the 1988 IMSA Camel Lights champion. He shared his four wins with co-driver David Loring (l.) in their Chevy-turned-Buick Tiga.
Photos/David Lubman (right), Sidell Tilghman (bottom).

That somebody turned out to be David Loring, a talented veteran heretofore cursed with the sort of racing budgets you could blow in one evening at Burger King. Further, when Hessert hired Loring to drive, he got an unexpected bonus. Loring, it turns out, is not only a fine driver; he's one hell of a teacher as well. By the time the team arrived at Daytona for the season's opener, Hessert was a much-improved driver—and that process continued all season. Hessert, Loring and Dave Simpson won the 24 Hours of Daytona in their Essex Racing Tiga-Chevrolet. The pair of Hessert and Loring then switched to Buick power and scored three more wins, at Sebring, West Palm Beach and Columbus. Coupled with a string of top-five finishes, that was enough to unseat the surprisingly winless three-time champion Jim Downing who, until Hessert wrapped up the title with a second at Del Mar, kept the pressure on with his usual consistency.

"I wouldn't have won it without him," Hessert said of Loring. Of his own progress as a driver, the new champion is modest: "I just wanted to be respected out there, wanted not to be called a wanker. I haven't beaten David yet, but I'm getting closer."

Hessert and Loring weren't the only stars in the Class of '88. Italy's Ruggero Melgrati showed plenty of speed in the Alba Ferrari he shared for part of the season with Martino Finotto, winning at Miami and Road Atlanta. Skeeter McKitterick won twice in a Whitehall Pontiac Firebird, solo at Lime Rock and with Costas Los at Watkins Glen, as did Charles Morgan, with Dominic Dobson at Mid-Ohio and solo at Portland. Four more strong Pontiac wins came from Formula Atlantic veteran—but IMSA rookie—Dan Marvin, who drove the Huffaker Firebird to victories at Elkhart Lake (with Terry Visger), Sears Point, San Antonio (with Bob Lobenberg) and Del Mar.

Those eight wins were more than enough to bring Pontiac the Lights manufacturers title. The series champion, though, is a man who now firmly believes rental cars are for airports: Cherry Hill, New Jersey's Tom Hessert.

IMSA rookie Dan Marvin took Camel Lights by storm in the Huffaker Racing Pontiac Firebird, by winning in every race he drove! Photo/Sidell Tilghman.

A fire after only two laps of the Sebring 12-hour race put an end to Chip Mead's efforts in John Higgins' Porsche Fabcar. Photo/Geoffrey Hewitt.

He didn't win a race in '88, but Jim Downing fought until the end for his fourth straight championship and lost it at the Del Mar finale. Photo/Al Steinberg.

Charles Morgan's two wins earned him fifth for the season. His efforts, combined with the high finishes of Skeeter McKitterick, Terry Visger and Dan Marvin brought the manufacturers title to Pontiac. Photo/Ken Brown-Competition Photographers.

Italy's Ruggero Melgrati showed plenty of speed in the Alba Ferrari (#80) he shared with Martino Finotto, winning at Miami and Road Atlanta. Photo/Sidell Tilghman.

Two Ferrari Albas were campaigned by Gaston Andrey. Uli Bieri had a less than successful season in #40. Photo/Ron McQueeney.

Scott Schubot and Linda
Ludemann shared a life and a
ride in their S & L Buick
Spice. Their best finish as a
duo was a fourth at Lime
Rock; Scott, driving alone,
scored seconds at Sears Point
and Portland. Photos/Sidell
Tilghman (top), W. H. Murenbeeld
(bottom).

Paul Lewis lost it at Lime Rock and
ended up on the tire wall. His driving
days for the Huffaker team were
numbered. Photo/Gene"Roz"Rosintoski.

The Ferrari Alba crew work on the pole-
sitting Finotto/Melgrati/Guido Dacco car
during a Sebring pit stop, where they
finished fourth. Photo/Rich Chenet.

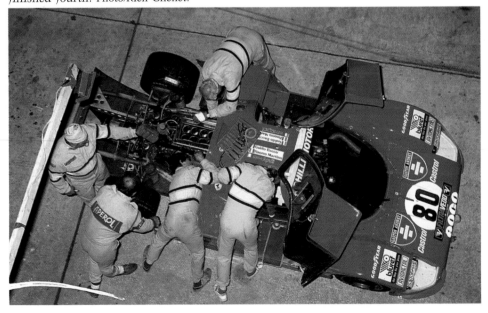

Whitehall Motorsports' Skeeter McKitterick won twice in a Pontiac Firebird, solo at Lime Rock and with Costas Los at Watkins Glen. Photo/Gene "Roz" Rosintoski.

Jim Downing kept the pressure on all season with his usual consistency in his Mazda Argo, scoring no wins but never finishing worse than seventh. After wearing it for three years, he relinquished his Camel Lights crown to Tom Hessert at the season finale. Photo/Werner Fritz.

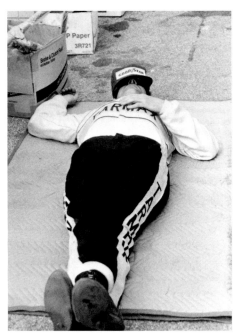

After a welcome nap, David Loring joined Tom Hessert in their Chevy Tiga to win the Daytona 24 Hours. Photo/Gene"Roz"Rosintoski.

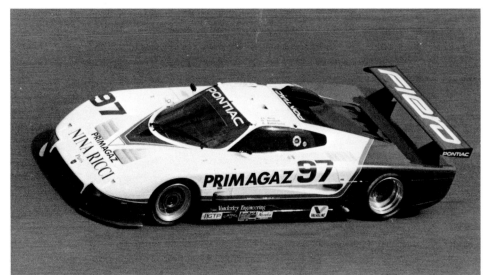

Teamed with Olin Jacobelli, Ballot-Lena and Ricci drove the #97 Whitehall Firebird at the Daytona 24 Hours. After 77 laps, they were out of the race. Photo/Geoffrey Hewitt.

Two Pontiac Firebirds were fielded by Whitehall Motorsports in '88. Skeeter McKitterick topped a roster of six drivers (including France's Claude Ballot-Lena and fragrance heir Jean Louis Ricci) with his two poles and two wins. Photo/Geoffrey Hewitt.

IMSA/Camel GTO

by GLENN HOWELL

WHEN *LAST WE LEFT THE* GTO division of the Camel GT series, it was the Toyota on top. Dan Gurney's turbocharged Celicas had successfully vanquished Ford and Chevrolet's V8 efforts in 1987.

For 1988, however, Ford upped the stakes dramatically by sending in the Jack Roush-prepared Merkur XR4Ti team—fresh from dominating the Trans-Am—to do GTO battle. Scott Pruett and Pete Halsmer had the drivers' seats and 2.5-liters of turbopower.

Chevrolet anted up as well, with Protofab Corvettes for Wally Dallenbach and, later, Greg Pickett. But the V8 bow tie brigade basically had to watch as the turbo cars swept by.

Truth be told, a somewhat strange quirk in the rules allowed the Merkurs to run a Ford V8 under the XR4Ti sheet metal, and Pruett/Halsmer started the season with a Daytona win in a Merkur V8 after being down some 35 laps at one point. This was followed by Dallenbach's Corvette V8 scoring at Sebring. But from then on it was a resumption of the turbo wars.

IMSA slapped Toyota with either additional weight or a smaller engine for 1988, and Gurney's All American Racers team opted for the smaller 2-liter engine. They even resorted to changing to the notchback Celica bodystyle as it allowed the rear spoiler to be two inches further back for more downforce. But they had met their match in the Merkurs and Pruett when it came to technology, engine power and driving talent.

"Consistency wins championships," noted Pruett, and although he had only a pair of wins it was four second places, a third and three fourths that nabbed him the GTO title and secured Lincoln-Mercury the manufacturers championship.

How competitive a year was it? Well, six drivers won the twelve GTO races...after Halsmer's three wins, everybody else scored a pair of victories (Halsmer and Pruett share credit for Daytona).

Defending champion Chris Cord was sidelined in mid-season with intestinal problems, at which point Dennis Aase stepped in to pair with Willy T. Ribbs on the Toyota team. Each of the Toyota drivers had two wins, and wound up splitting a lot of points between themselves. They fought hard and tough, but were ultimately lacking in the reliability that gave Pruett the title. Both the team and its drivers move on to GTP next season, Toyota departing from GTO.

Dallenbach posted relatively consistent top-10 finishes in the Protofab-prepared Corvette, and finished as runner-up in the standings. He, too, is also moving on from the series. The same IMSA rules which allowed V8 Merkurs also allowed V6 Corvettes. The Protofab team tried the blown route with a turbocharged V6 at mid-season for Pickett, but it was even less reliable than the 5.5-liter V8 and they just ran out of what few motors they had.

Mazda's foray into the world of big bucks and big motors was less than successful with Roger Mandeville soldiering on to several top-10 finishes in his triple-rotor RX7, a pair of thirds his best all season.

While Pruett moves to Indy cars, Halsmer will stay with the Roush team as it converts the cars to Cougars (the Merkur XR4Ti is fini in the United States) and develops a NASCAR-based V6 racing engine for the '89 season.

A new factor will be introduced in 1989 when Nissan makes a major effort in GTO, going head to head with Mercury and Chevrolet. Driver Steve Millen has been spirited away from Toyota and the Clayton Cunningham Racing team away from Mazda to run the new effort.

Best GTO Race of the Year: without doubt, the Del Mar finale—a glorious, clean race between Ribbs and Pruett. They've had their rough moments both on and off the track, but here they showed that both of them have matured into top-notch racing drivers.

The 1988 IMSA Camel GTO Champion, Scott Pruett. Photo/Stan Clinton.

Roger Mandeville skipped the last two races, placing sixth in GTO points for Mazda. His best finishes in an underpowered car were a pair of thirds. Photo/Randy McKee.

Wally Dallenbach matched Scott Pruett's two victories, but was left standing on the corner for the championship. He ended up second, 44 points down. Photo/W. H. Murenbeeld.

While Scott Pruett moves to Indy cars in '89, Pete Halsmer will stay with the Roush team as it converts the cars to Cougars (the Merkur XR4Ti is fini in the U.S.). Pruett's victories, and Halsmer's solo wins at West Palm Beach and Portland, helped Lincoln-Mercury capture the '88 manufacturers title. Photo/Jim Phillipson.

The same IMSA rules which allowed V8 Merkurs also allowed V6 Corvettes. The Polyvoltac/Protofab team tried the blown route with a turbocharged V6 at mid-season for Greg Pickett, but it was even less reliable than the 5.5-liter V8 that Wally Dallenbach drove. Photo/David Taylor.

Dan Gurney's (r.) protege, Willy T. Ribbs, placed third in points for Toyota. Photo/Al Steinberg.

Porsche's best entry in GTO racing in '88 was Chet Vincentz' Porsche 944T, out of Alexandria, Virginia. Photo/Ken Brown-Competition Photographers.

A strange quirk in IMSA's rules allowed the Merkurs to run a Ford V8 under the XR4Ti sheet metal. The '87 championship-winning Toyotas met their match in '88 in the Merkurs and Pruett when it came to technology, engine power, and driving talent. Photo/Jim Hatfield.

Only fourth in points, Pete Halsmer scored the most wins for the year for Lincoln-Mercury—three. Photo/Randy McKee.

Dan Gurney's All-American Racers Toyota Celica bounced off the guardrail a few times in practice, but driver Dennis Aase came back after repairs to win the Watkins Glen race, then finished fifth for the year. Photo/Randy McKee.

Defending champion Chris Cord was sidelined in mid-season with intestinal problems after a win at Mid-Ohio, then came back to win again at Columbus, ending up seventh for the season. Photo/Randy McKee.

For 1988, Ford upped the stakes dramatically by sending in the Jack Roush-prepared Merkur XR4Ti team—fresh from dominating the Trans-Am—to do GTO battle with 2.5 liters of turbopower. Photo/Jim Hatfield.

Recuperated from a testing crash in '87, Dennis Aase returned to GTO to replace the ailing Chris Cord, scoring two wins. Photo/Randy McKee.

Jack Baldwin and Buz McCall teamed up to drive the Skoal Bandit Camaro. McCall took a second at Daytona, Baldwin matched it at West Palm Beach. Photo/Randy McKee.

FOR SOME PEOPLE, THERE WAS NO DROUGHT THIS SUMMER.

LINCOLN-MERCURY CONTINUES TO REIGN, WINNING ITS FIFTH STRAIGHT MANUFACTURER'S CUP.

On the 1988 GTO circuit, one race team left the others feeling all wet. Scott Pruett and Pete Halsmer, driving race-prepared XR4Tis, won four races, amassed 185 points, and clinched the 1988 IMSA Camel GTO Manufacturer's Championship for Lincoln-Mercury.

The championship is the third straight for the XR4Ti race team, winners on the Trans Am circuit in 1986 and 1987, and it caps a most impressive debut season in GTO. Combined with

Mercury Capri's winning years in Trans Am, this year's championship is the fifth consecutive Manufacturer's Cup for Lincoln-Mercury.

XR4Ti driver Scott Pruett kept his personal winning streak alive by winning a second straight Driver's Championship. He and teammate Pete Halsmer emerged victorious on some of the circuit's toughest courses: at Daytona Beach, Portland, West Palm Beach, and Summit Point.

The XR4Ti team enjoyed the sponsorship

of Mac Tools and Stroh, and was helped by an EEC-IV engine management system from Ford Electronics, makers of the performance-enhancing EEC-IV systems in Lincoln-Mercury's production vehicles.

The turbocharged XR4Ti sports coupe from Germany. When it reigns, it pours it on. Test-drive the 175-horsepower street version at select Lincoln-Mercury dealers. **For more information, call 1-800-822-9292.**

LINCOLN-MERCURY
MOTORSPORT

LINCOLN-MERCURY DIVISION *Ford*
Buckle up—together we can save lives.

IMSA/Camel GTU

by GLENN HOWELL

TECHNOLOGY TOOK TWO giant steps forward in IMSA's GTU ranks in 1988, and the new cars and their engineering advances left a lot of people scrambling in a class that had been one of the least expensive in professional sports car racing. After being a foreign car playground for all of its 18-year history, it was the domestic manufacturers who raised the level of competition so dramatically by the end of the year.

Two-time and defending champion Tom Kendall was either very lucky or very astute when he jumped from his title-winning Mazda RX7 into the new, high-tech, V6-powered Chevrolet Beretta. With a win at Miami in its first event (the Cars and Concepts team skipped the Daytona 24-hour grind), Kendall then added five more wins including the final three races of the season to take his third GTU title in as many years.

At 21, Tom Kendall became only the third driver in IMSA history to win a third straight Camel GT championship. By scoring six victories in 11 starts, he became the 1988 IMSA Camel GTU Champion—again. Photo/Sidell Tilghman.

His record speaks not only for the Chevy's ability to hang together, but for his ability to finish well—only once did he finish out of the top 10 in 11 events, and only twice out of the top five in those same races. He and teammate Max Jones combined to give the manufacturers title to Chevrolet, as well, in its first year of GTU competition.

"I wouldn't have made the jump if I didn't think we had a chance at the championship," said Kendall. The Chevrolets, with the 3-liter V6 and advanced chassis and aerodynamics simply moved the whole class—which, for the previous eight years, had been a Mazda private preserve—forward a notch. Jones had one win in his Cars and Concepts entry, and finished third in GTU standings within a heartbeat of Amos Johnson.

Amos Johnson won the biggies, the Daytona 24 Hours and the Sebring 12 Hours in a Mazda RX7, but failed to do better than second once the Berettas came along. The popular veteran driver from Raleigh, North Carolina, was runner-up in the points chase. Photo/Sidell Tilghman.

Johnson rallied the rotary troops behind him with endurance wins at both Daytona and Sebring in his Mazda RX7, but it was tough going the rest of the year as the Mazdas were out-powered and out-handled. The rotary reliability, and sheer number of Mazda entries, provided plenty of manufacturer points and a distant hope of taking that title for the ninth time until it was quashed with a Chevy win at Del Mar which saw Kendall nudge Johnson's new RX7 into the wall, whereupon it crossed the track and was destroyed in a two car collision with the third place runner.

Interestingly enough, it was Dodge which seized the Chevy gauntlet, assigning to Kal Showket's operation the building of two ultra-lightweight 2.5-liter Daytonas for himself and Dorsey Schroeder. The cars were a little late getting started, but broke new ground as they tipped the scales at a svelte 1650 pounds—the Chevy's had to lug around an additional 450 pounds.

Showket's front-wheel drive version wasn't up to beating the Chevys and will be abandoned in '89, but Schroeder's rear-drive version hit its stride in mid-season, taking three wins in four races.

Pontiac had pulled the plug on the Fiero racing effort, and although there were valiant private entries the lack of money for development showed as the car was simply no longer a winner.

Mid-season spice was provided by Don Reynolds, a brave man who works for Electramotive...the people who bring you the Nissan GTP car. With a discarded V6 block sleeved down to two-liters, he installed the turbomotor in an evil-handling Nissan 280ZX and proceeded to show everyone what real horsepower was all about. Although it was a swan song for this particular car as turbos are banned from GTU in 1989, Nissan will be back with an increased presence next season.

Best GTU Race of the Year: it has to be Portland where Reynolds' Nissan scared the devil out of the major teams, Max Jones finally got his first win, and Schroeder turned in another fine drive for third behind Kendall.

From Long Beach, California, Max Jones. Photo/Randy McKee.

Max Jones drove a second Chevrolet Beretta, taking one solo win at Portland, to place third in points. Photo/Kenneth F. Hawking.

The relatively-unknown Dorsey Schroeder caused head-scratching in the Chevy camp when he showed up in a svelte Dodge Daytona and out-performed the Berettas on too many occasions for their taste. Dorsey won three races, ending up fifth in points. Photo/Randy McKee.

Amos Johnson rallied the rotary troops behind him with his endurance wins, but it was tough going the rest of the year. Mazda, however, remains the all-time Camel GT-winning car with 94 wins over Porsche Carrera's 68. Photo/Bill Stahl.

It came down to the final race at Del Mar. The war for the manufacturers championship was being waged for the last time. Mazda brought all the artillery they could muster up. Chevrolet put Bart Kendall in a third Beretta. After 30 harrowing, metal-banging laps, the dust settled and the battle-scarred Chevrolet of Tom Kendall emerged the victor, marking the first time a domestic car maker has won a GTU manufacturers title in the class' 18-year history. Photo/Sidell Tilghman.

Longtime Nissan driver
George Alderman drove in
only two races.
Photo/Randy McKee.

This spin on Summit Point's slippery
post-rain surface didn't keep Tom Kendall
out of the victory circle. Photo/Randy McKee.

One of Nissan's hopes for a GTU success
was in the hands of Morris Clement in
George Alderman's Nissan 300ZX.
Photo/Ken Brown-Competition Photographers.

Mid-Ohio hosted
one of Tom
Kendall's six
victories for
Chevrolet.
Photo/Jim Hatfield.

113

Another candidate for a Nissan win in '88 was Bob Leitzinger. Although often very fast, reliability was not the car's strong point. Photo/Ken Brown-Competition Photographers.

With a discarded V6 block sleeved down to two liters, Don Reynolds of Electramotive (builders of the Nissan GTP car) installed the soon-to-be-banned turbo motor in a 280ZX and proceeded to blow the doors off the competition at three events. He sat on the pole twice, but never won. Photo/Randy McKee.

Yes, Tom Kendall, you're still number one. Photo/Stan Clinton.

A second at Summit Point was Al Bacon's best finish all season for Mazda. He was sixth in points. Photo/Ken Brown-Competition Photographers.

IMSA/American Challenge

by KEITH WALTZ
ASSOCIATE EDITOR, *NATIONAL SPEED SPORT NEWS*

WHEN *THE FINAL CHECKERED* flag was waved on the 1987 International Motor Sports Association's American Challenge series, Dick Danielson was broken-hearted. The Heartland, Wisconsin auto mechanic entered that final event with a one-point margin in the title chase over defending series champion Irv Hoerr. But Hoerr beat Danielson to the finish line by a mere four seconds and won the championship by an equally mere four points.

Nineteen-eighty-seven was not Dick Danielson's year. But 1988 turned out to be much better.

With Hoerr now competing regularly on the Sports Car Club of America's Escort Trans-Am circuit and with an ex-Hoerr Oldsmobile Toronado under him, Danielson was the class of IMSA's "muscle car" division. The 34-year-old driver, who had finished second, third and fourth in the series standings the last three years, won three of the five races en route to claiming his first championship trophy.

The campaign opened with Danielson nipping Clay Young's Pontiac Firebird by .8-second at Connecticut's Lime Rock Park in late May. Many series insiders were betting the championship would come down to a battle between Danielson and Young and the first race made their bets look pretty sure.

In August, a torrential downpour just minutes before the start of Round Two at New York's famed Watkins Glen made things quite interesting. Danielson and Young were both involved in a first turn, first lap accident which heavily damaged Young's Pontiac, ending his day and leaving him in 22nd spot. Danielson made several pit stops without losing a lap during the resulting caution period to repair his damaged car and he rejoined the battle, minus his front-end sheetmetal.

Former series champ Craig Carter, in his only American Challenge appearance of the season, went on to win the event, but Danielson put on a show as he charged from the rear of the pack to finish second in his "air conditioned" Olds. Patty Moise, who left the series at the end of 1987 to concentrate on NASCAR stock car racing, made a rare appearance and finished third.

After 24 cars were on hand for the Watkins Glen round, only eight showed for Round Three, held in the streets of San Antonio, Texas in early September. Danielson survived two scrapes, including an early spin, to record his fifth career AC victory. Danielson made up a 12-second deficit, taking the lead from Young on lap 13 of the 24-lap event. Young brought his Pontiac home second and Mark Porcaro was third.

Dick Danielson, the 1988 American Challenge champion, drove an Olds Toronado to three wins in five races. Photo/Ken Brown-Competition Photographers.

It was back to Watkins Glen for race number four, but this time things were not nearly as chaotic. Danielson posted a wire-to-wire victory and when Young went crashing into the Turn Ten tire wall in the early laps, the championship battle was over. Steve Clark finished second in a Buick Somerset and Wayne Darling took third in a Chevrolet Camaro.

The series finale, part of the inaugural World Challenge of Tampa, came in late November on a temporary street circuit at the Florida State Fairgrounds. Hoerr returned for the finale and easily won the event in an Oldsmobile Toronado which had spent most of the year as a show car. Danielson finished second to his old rival and Clark was third.

Danielson took the title by a whopping 38 points over Darling who recorded two thirds, two fourths and one fifth. Young, also failing to go the distance in Tampa, was third in the final standings. Clark, with three top-10 finishes, was fourth and Mark Porcaro took fifth with four top-10 showings.

Oldsmobile once again claimed the manufacturers championship and Danielson earned the Norelco Cup for his outstanding driving performances during the season.

Following her third-place finish at Watkins Glen, Moise was named the series' top woman driver and Darling was selected as the most improved.

As the year closed, the future of the American Challenge series was somewhat clouded. Some insiders said the series may compete as a separate class in IMSA's GTO and GTU series, with the addition of several stand-alone events in future years.

But no matter what the future holds for the American Challenge, 1988 was Dick Danielson's year.

As Dan Osterholt slips off the course, Steve Clark, Dick Danielson and Jerry Sarnataro proceed onward. Photo/Ken Brown-Competition Photographers.

Top-five finishes in every race assured Wayne Darling of second place in the championship. Photo/ Stan Clinton.

Driving a Chevrolet Beretta, Mark Porcaro edged into fifth for the year, just one point better than Tom Forgione. San Antonio saw Porcaro's best finish, a third. Photo/Ken Brown-Competition Photographers.

Clay Young survived several scrapes to claim third spot in the standings. Photo/Stan Clinton.

IMSA/International Sedan Cup

by KEITH WALTZ
ASSOCIATE EDITOR, *NATIONAL SPEED SPORT NEWS*

AFTER *ROOKIE SENSATION* Parker Johnstone made a shambles of the 1987 International Sedan Series, officials of IMSA revised the rules for the small-car road racing series. Many insiders felt the changes were an effort to prevent a Honda Acura runaway in 1988. Following a 1-2 Mazda finish in the 1988 opener at Georgia's Road Atlanta, it appeared as if the goal may well have been accomplished. But things are not always as they seem.

Driving his red CompuTech Acura Integra, Johnstone overcame the new rules and went on to win six of the 10 races en route to his second straight series championship.

In addition to the new specifications, after running on a single brand of rubber the previous year the series also played host to a heated tire war, BFGoodrich, Yokohama and Toyo participated in the battle for bragging rights.

The first half of the season was a five-car show with the Acuras of Johnstone and teammate Doug Peterson, and the Mazdas of Amos Johnson, Dennis Shaw and Dave Jolly stealing the spotlight.

Johnson won the Road Atlanta opener with Johnstone coming back from a fourth-place finish in the debut to win Round Two on a temporary circuit in West Palm Beach, Florida.

Race number three at West Virginia's Summit Point Raceway saw Jolly hold off Peterson to post Mazda's second victory of the campaign. Johnstone started from pole position and was well in command, but after 12 laps his Acura suddenly lost power, relegating him to 20th position.

The next round took the troops to Connecticut's Lime Rock Park where Johnson beat Johnstone to the checkered flag by a mere 1.7 seconds. Then Round Five saw Johnstone hold off Johnson for victory number two.

But after that fifth race at Mid-Ohio, one IMSA official was heard to say, "This is the last of the five-car races." A five percent weight penalty was announced for the ProFormance cars, specifically the Acuras and the Mazdas.

But as it turned out, the weight penalty was a great idea for the Acuras as it put them into the next poundage category, allowing them to run two more inches of rubber. And even though the rule-makers later added more weight to the two Japanese makes, a change which also allowed the Mazdas to run bigger tires, the Acura team went on to win each of the five remaining races.

After his Mid-Ohio triumph, Johnstone was victorious at Watkins Glen, Road America and Portland International Raceway. He clinched the title in California with an August victory at Sears Point International Raceway.

As things turned out, it was a good thing the title was in hand prior to the series' finale on the downtown streets of Columbus, Ohio, as a bump sent Johnstone crashing into the wall early in the race. With Johnstone out of action, teammate Peterson upheld the Acura honors, winning his first race since the season opener in 1987.

Johnson, with two victories and four seconds, settled for runner-up honors in the championship battle. Peterson took third, Shaw claimed fourth and Dave Jolly rounded out the top five in the final point standings.

The 1988 International Sedan Cup champion, Parker Johnstone (c.), shares some bubbly with teammate Doug Peterson (l.) and Dennis Shaw (r.) after their top-three finish at Watkins Glen. Photo/Tom Bernhardt.

Amos Johnson, with two victories and four seconds in a Mazda 323, settled for runner-up honors in the championship battle. Photo/ Geoffrey Hewitt.

Bob Strange, widely recognized for his BFGoodrich television commercials, came home "first in class," driving a Mercedes 190 "luxury sedan" prepared by Rick Hirst Racing. Only a disqualification for a mechanical infraction at Summit Point kept Strange from having a perfect top-10 finishing record. He ended up sixth in the final standings.

Veteran road racer Lance Stewart joined the Acura team in a third car for the final three races, posting two thirds and one sixth-place finish to take seventh in points.

Acura claimed the manufacturers championship with Mazda second and Mercedes third. On the strength of its showings on the Acuras and the Mercedes, BFGoodrich earned the tire manufacturer championship with Yokohama second and Toyo a distant third.

Johnstone also received the Norelco Driver's Cup for his season-long performance and he shared the LuK Fastest Qualifier award with Amos Johnson.

In just two years on the circuit, Johnstone has won 13 races of the 20 held. He began his racing career in 1977 driving autocross events before moving into the road racing arena. The Novato, California resident went on to win the 1985 IMSA Renault Cup title and then claimed the 1986 SCCA GT-4 championship. Coupled with his two straight IS crowns, Johnstone has now won national titles in each of the last four racing seasons.

Quite an accomplishment.

Driving his red CompuTech Acura Integra, Johnstone overcame IMSA's new rules revisions and went on to win six of the 10 races en route to his second straight series championship. Photo/Sidell Tilghman.

The series title was already decided prior to the series finale on the downtown streets of Columbus, Ohio, as a bump sent Johnstone crashing into the wall. Teammate Doug Peterson upheld the Acura honors, winning his first race since the season opener in 1987. Photo/Mark Windecker.

119

The Dodge boys, with Dorsey Schroeder, Neil Hanneman and film star Bobby Carradine behind the wheels of their Shelby CSXs, charged ahead with their development program, despite mid-pack performances. Photo/Geoffrey Hewitt.

Piloting Mazda 323s, Dennis Shaw (#6) and Dave Jolly were fourth and fifth, respectively, in points. Photo/Geoffrey Hewitt.

Bob Strange, widely recognized for his BFGoodrich TV commercials, drove a Mercedes 190 "luxury sedan." Only a disqualification for a mechanical infraction at Summit Point kept Strange from having a perfect top-10 finishing record. He ended up sixth. Photo/Sidell Tilghman.

Doug Peterson landed in third place for the season, helping garner enough points, with Johnstone, for Acura to claim the manufacturers title. Photo/Tom Bernhardt.

IMSA/Firestone Firehawk Endurance Championship

by BOB AKIN

I CAN'T BELIEVE I'M DOING *this again. This is my 24th 24-hour race. These long races are exhausting, expensive, and require discipline to drive at an assigned pace suppressing the urge to race with almost everyone who comes along. I've never won a 24-hour race, although I've led a few, finished second at Daytona (twice), fourth at Le Mans and did fairly well in some others. But now, at Watkins Glen on June 12, 1988, after 23 hours of racing; the fitful sleep, hurry-up meals, a midnight driving stint and another drive into the blazing dawn, I sense we are going to win.*

In 1988, IMSA's Firestone Firehawk Endurance Championship grew still more competitive although the Camaro/Firebird teams continued to dominate. Porsches were permitted to use the 944S four-valve engine in place of last year's two-valve version. Selected GM teams got better brakes and other subtle goodies. The BMW M-3s went faster as did the Nissan 300 ZX Turbos, although IMSA's jiffy "instant on" tell-tale boost gauge kept the Mazda rotary muffler boys fairly honest. Everyone went a few second's quicker than in 1987.

In 1988, Joe Varde, of Tampa, Florida, locked up the Firestone Firehawk Grand Sports drivers championship for himself and the manufacturers title for Pontiac. Photo/Stan Clinton.

There was the usual fender (and car) bending, which is an unfortunate way of life in Firehawk. Although it seems the most experienced drivers have the fewest dents, everyone regards this racing as a "Contact Sport." Yet, given the equality of the cars, the generally large fields and the ferocious competition, some mishaps are inevitable.

The series began at Sebring, Florida in March and ranged the length and breadth of America, ending in Tampa on Thanksgiving weekend. By then, local hero Joe Varde had locked up the Grand Sports Championship for Pontiac (Joe's original Camaro got a nose job just before Elkhart Lake and became a Firebird). In the final Grand Sports standings, GM cars held the top nine spots

with the Korman/Lewis BMW M-3 hanging on for 10th. The Akin/White Racing team of six 944Ss had some good runs, led often and certainly populated the fields with little red cars, but a win was not in the cards for us in '88.

Norris Rancourt claimed the Sports Division championship for Honda in his CRX-Si and while dozens of Volkswagon GTIs assured VW of the Touring Class Trophy, Paul Hacker had to sweat out the driving championship right down to the last race.

The Watkins Glen 24 Hour Firehawk event was the best 24-hour race I've ever run. We led for five hours and 40 minutes of the last six hours. In the end, the Camaros caught us. We lost by 41 seconds. There's some tough, close racing in this Firehawk Series!

Chet Edwards in the King Kondom Camaro found Lime Rock's Big Bend to be stiff competition and lost it in the dirt. Photo/Gene"Roz"Rosintoski.

Mike Speakman kissed the guardrail during the 24-hour Watkins Glen race, proceeded to turn over once, then added a

half twist and slid on his roof before his Nissan finally came to rest, his Firestone Firehawks spinning in the breeze. Needless to

Nighttime in Columbus. Streaked headlights compete with a lit-up Government building during the night race through the streets of the Ohio capitol. Photo/Mark Windecker.

Norris Rancourt, teamed with John Green, topped the Sports Division in his Honda CRX-Si. Runner-up Terry Earwood equalled his three wins with a Dodge Daytona, but lost the championship by 55 points! Photo/Stan Clinton.

The Akin/White Racing team of six 944Ss had some good runs, led often and certainly populated the fields with little red cars, but a win was not in the cards. Photo/Gene "Roz" Rosintoski.

say, he was out of the race after only 19 laps of a 553-lap event. *Photos/Gene "Roz" Rosintoski.*

123

IMSA/Firestone Firehawk Enduro

While dozens of Volkswagen GTIs assured VW of the Touring class trophy, Paul Hacker had to sweat out the driving championship right down to the last race. Here he and brother Karl stay close to achieve a good draft down the straight. Photo/Ken Brown-Competition Photographers.

Oldsmobile's mid-season entry into the Touring class from the Sports division proved powerful. An Olds won each of the last three races and came in second in the manufacturers championship. Photo/Ken Brown-Competition Photographers.

Tied for third in Grand Sports were teammates Leighton Reese and Brad Hoyt, who drove the highest-placing Camaro. Photo/Stan Clinton.

Toyotas filled out the fields in both Sports and Touring, but none made it into the top 10. Photo/Ken Brown-Competition Photographers.

SCCA/Escort Endurance Championship

by TONY SWAN
AUTOMOTIVE EDITOR, *POPULAR MECHANICS*

*I**F THE MEASURE OF A RACING* season is how close things stand going into the final event, then the 1988 SCCA Escort Endurance Championship measured up very well indeed. When the tour rolled into Sebring, the last date on an eight-race calendar, the issue was still very much in doubt for two of three class championships.

But when the checkered flag finally fell—or, to be historically accurate, one lap before it fell—all the titles were decided. The disputed overtime lap, which was disallowed, could have given one of the Saleen Autosport Mustangs a second straight series title, but as it turned out the Morrison-Cook Camaro of John Heinricy and Don Knowles brought the crown back to Chevyville. Another Morrison-Cook Camaro (Stu Hayner/Bob McConnell) was second in the season standings. Hayner also scored the most drivers points in the GT class.

The Morrison-Cook Camaro team of John Heinricy (r.) and Don Knowles (l.) took top honors in the GT class of the 1988 Escort Endurance Championship. Their successes in their Camaro brought back the manufacturers crown to Chevyville. Photos/Sidell Tilghman.

Another Morrison-Cook Camaro for Stu Hayner and Bob McConnell was second in the season standings. Hayner also scored the most driver's points in the GT class. Photo/Art Flores.

The battle in SSB was just as close, with a Honda CRX Si (Lance Stewart, P.D. Cunningham) from John Torok's Team GRR and a Phoenix Racing VW GTI (Bill Pate, Peter Schwartzott) dead even going into Sebring. Although neither of the Jackson Racing-prepared Torok Hondas was able to win, both came home ahead of the Phoenix Racing car to cinch first and third for the season. Cunningham was the top B driver, followed closely by teammate Ed Conner, and Team GRR won six of the eight races.

Pepe Pombo and Scott Sharp dominated the SSA class in their Nissan 300ZX, with seven wins in eight races. Nissan also took the SSA class manufacturers title. Photo/Sidell Tilghman.

The SSB class championship was a dusty battle right to the last race, among the Team GRR Hondas and the Phoenix Racing VW GTI. Photo/Jim Hatfield.

The SSB class championship was a dusty battle right to the last race, among the Team GRR Hondas and the Phoenix Racing VW GTI. Photo/Jim Hatfield.

Class A was the only cakewalk, as wily Pepe Pombo captained a campaign that was all but perfect, taking class honors in seven races and second place in the other. Pombo shared his Nissan 300 ZX primarily with Scott Sharp, with Ray Kong lending a hand in the longer races.

As you'd expect, manufacturer titles paralleled the team championships, Chevy winning GT, Nissan taking SSA and Honda claiming SSB. In the tire wars, Goodyear had the edge in GT but General-shod entries won in both SSA and SSB.

Chevrolet Camaros dominated the GT class, with two Morrison-Cook cars topping the class championship. Here, at Brainerd, a total of eight lead changes occurred with the two teams combining to lead 55 of the 89 race laps, including the last 37. The #98 team of McConnell-Hayner won. Photo/Sidell Tilghman.

Bob McConnell drove a
Morrison-Cook Camaro to
second in the GT class team
standings and also to second
in driver's points.
Photo/Sidell Tilghman.

The #42 Team GRR Honda driven by Lance Stewart and Peter
Cunningham came out on top in the SSB class championship
chase by finishing second in the final race at Sebring.
Photo/Sidell Tilghman.

The Phoenix Racing team of Bill Pate
and Peter Schwartzott was tied in the
SSB class with the Team GRR Honda
CRX team going into the final race. Their
sixth-place finish there dropped them
into second spot for the season.
Photo/Art Flores.

SCCA/Corvette Challenge

by LAURA CULLEY

WHEN YOU PUT 40 IDENTICAL Corvettes together on the same race track with some of America's most talented drivers going after a total million-dollar purse, you better expect fireworks. That's just what the brand new Corvette Challenge delivered.

After 10 races featuring some of the closest competition imaginable, Californian Stu Hayner banked a $142,800 paycheck. And he only won once. He did, however, make a total of four winner's circle visits with his Mobil 1/Tom Bell Chevrolet-sponsored Corvette. With elbow room at a premium, the key to winning this series was consistency. Hayner finished out of the top 10 only once which give him a narrow 17-point margin over Juan Manuel Fangio II.

Fangio, in the Manliba/Gloy Sports entry, also visited the winner's circle four times, including a series-high three wins occurring at Riverside, Portland and the Meadowlands. He finished just out of the top 10 three times which was enough to give him second overall.

Four drivers juggled the points lead. Actor/race driver Bobby Carradine jumped out to an early lead in his Mobil 1/Tom Bell Chevrolet-sponsored Corvette but mechanical woes set in which bumped him back to mid-field. Shawn Hendricks (Spot-Not Car Wash/Valley Chevrolet/MPA Motorsports) cut into the series lead at Riverside, holding it until the Meadowlands when luck turned against him. There, Fangio took over with his third win but just when it began to look like Fangio was unassailable, Hayner's top-10 roll began to pay off. He grabbed the lead with a last-lap win at Mosport and held on through the season finale.

After 10 races featuring some of the closest competition imaginable, Californian Stu Hayner banked a $142,800 paycheck and won the 1988 Corvette Challenge drivers championship in his Tom Bell Chevrolet-sponsored car. Photo/Art Flores.

At season's end, the Corvette Challenge's only three-time Indy winner, Johnny Rutherford, was given the 1988 Mid-America Sportsman Award. Rutherford, who never finished better than 15th, said, "Boy, did I learn a lot about showroom stock racing!" Photo/Ron McQueeney.

Another celebrity, Bruce Jenner, had a tough time of it in Corvette Challenge, with an 11th at Riverside his best for the year. Photo/Ken Brown-Competition Photographers.

After wallowing in the middle of the field for most of the season, GTP racer Doc Bundy finally took a fourth at the last race at St. Pete. Photo/Ken Brown-Competition Photographers.

Rising star Juan Fangio II won three times, two more than Hayner, yet ended up second, 17 points back. Photo/Rich Fercy.

They say rain equalizes drivers' performances. Perhaps not. Here, at rainy Mid-Ohio, driving styles varied. Photo/Trackside Photo.

130

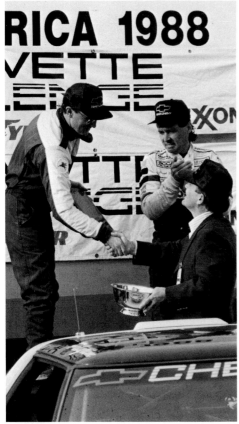

At Road America, winner Andy Pilgrim received his trophy from his sponsor, John Bergstrom of Bergstrom Chevrolet. Series champion Stuart Hayner (r.) was second. Pilgrim was fourth for the year.
Photo/Rich Fercy.

Brotherly teamwork is the trademark of the Tommy and Bobby Archer duo, but Bobby's season was a dismal one, with only two top-five finishes earned.
Photo/Ken Brown-Competition Photographers.

Juan Fangio II (#2) and Tommy Archer splashed through the puddles at Mid-Ohio. Fangio placed third while Archer claimed his second season win to take a third in points. Photo/Sidell Tilghman.

No one dominated this series, and the grid was proof. Event after event, about 20 Corvettes were stuffed within the same second on the grid. Photo/Art Flores.

Mark Behm switched to Corvette Challenge after a successful season in VW Golf Cup competition. But the transition from front-wheel-drive to rear-wheel-power proved a handful. Behm never reached the top 10.
Photo/Rich Fercy.

Commentary:

DOES THE FUTURE OF THE SPORT RUN IN THE STREETS? SHOULD IT?

by PETE LYONS

I'M IN A STRANGE CITY striding down a sidewalk to a business appointment. At an intersection, I'm halted by a crossing light. I look around. My eye settles on something odd—something profoundly disturbing.

Black streaks on the street. Tire marks, but they are no usual ones. Sweeping diagonally across the normal flow of traffic, brushing close in to the curb at my feet, they describe a free-form arc utterly alien to the regimented pattern of the city. No familiar, everyday vehicle could follow such a path without creating enormous carnage.

My scalp feels suddenly cold. What terrifying anarchy has been unleashed here?

No, I haven't stumbled across an auto racing street circuit I didn't know about, but the way things are going it could happen. So many temporary tracks of this sort have sprung up in the past decade, all over North America, that it almost seems to be the way of the future in auto racing. I view this with understanding, and some fondness. But I can't shake some feelings of misgiving.

I do admit to many positive aspects of street circuits. First, as we all know too well, racing is a difficult enthusiasm to cultivate. Taking the show to the fans can benefit the sport as a whole, particularly if it winds up making new fans from townsfolk who would never have bothered to seek out the traditional racing locations.

Second, I think, should be listed the glamour factor. Precisely because it seems so outrageous, staging a race inside a city attracts the attention that interests sponsors.

Then there's the convenience for many—though not all—of those involved, from the local media, who merely have to step outdoors to cover the event, to the competitors, who, for once, can enjoy comfortable hotels within minutes of the pits.

Nor can we overlook the fact that, in many parts of the continent, a raceway made of city streets is the only raceway available. Real racers will, and have, run anywhere—horse tracks, farm fields, logging roads, constructions sites, mine workings, parking lots, airports, deserts, dry lakes, salt flats, beaches—but when you're desperate for a place to race, turning to city streets makes a good deal of sense.

In a way, too, running competition cars on public streets seems right. After all, auto racing's roots are in the road. Preserving a link to the pioneer days retains some of the sport's original relevance to everyday cars.

There are certain aesthetic qualities that are best appreciated in a round-the-houses race. Sound, for instance. At Monte Carlo, there are places deep in the "canyons" between the towering buildings where the cars set up a hollow reverberation that send goosebumps along your spine. At Long Beach, in some years, the course has run through a huge, tunnel-like structure that concentrates the noise to a deliciously ear-splitting intensity.

Similarly, all racing presents a fine sense of desperate peril that is nicely brought out by a street circuit. When you see a smoking-hot rear tire just brush a barrier, tearing the banner draped over it but not touching the steel or cement behind, you realize you've seen either unbeliveable precision or incredible luck.

And no place gives you a better feeling for a top-line race car's astonishing performance. Geared tight for the lap, out of the turns it will spin its wheels, cock sideways and then dig in and accelerate away almost faster than you can swing your eye to follow it.

Positive aspects granted, however, we must also acknowledge the negative ones. Lined with ugly crash barriers, today's street courses tend to be narrow and bumpy, the lap is generally too tight and slow to be very interesting, and few of them afford the public better than a mediocre view. From the competitors' viewpoint, pit and paddock facilities are often barely adequate, the nature of the track causes a high number of accidents and breakdowns, and safety is often compromised both by the restricted vision past the cement walls and by the difficulty of removing a derelict car from between them.

Other problems that have affected me personally at street courses include inadequate parking, long walks between, say, press room and pits, and restricted photo sites.

Then too, the Purist in me feels revulsion about the "Meaning of it All." I suspect that some of these annual events are put on in localities where racing is less an enthusiast tradition than a bald-faced commercial enterprise. The promoters sometimes have nothing else to do with the sport, and may be entirely oblivious of its heritage and indifferent to its future. One fairly recent example was a casino's attempt to make a Las Vegas parking lot a classic racing venue. I thought it was the rankest prostitution to stage a Grand Prix there. I'm glad the scheme failed.

Once-a-year tracks also suggest disturbing

implications about the welfare of racing in years to come. After all, if the lucrative events all move to street circuits, how will the dedicated permanent facilities survive, and where, then, will future drivers learn their trade?

It is true that the race drivers of the distant past learned on nothing but temporary courses. Formal auto racing began on public highways closed—sometimes barely—for the occasion. Some of these venues lasted into modern times. I arrived relatively late on the scene, but I have vivid personal memories of closed-road courses at Barcelona, Bridgehampton, Pau, Sicily and Spa, among others. Of course, Monte Carlo's hilly streets have an indelible place in racing history, and don't forget that most of Le Mans' Mulsanne Straight is still a five-kilometer section of everyday French highway. These two sites host two of the most important races in the world, their stature not stunted in the least by their being available only once a year.

The purpose-built artificial tracks, both ovals and road circuits, are the newcomers. They came along with good reason. They offered places to race when the great town-to-town events were closed down. They were safer and more convenient for both the competitors and the general public. They allowed the promoters to better control the spectators, and thus to build racing as a legitimate business. They made possible driving schools to bring along the beginners in an orderly, efficient way, as well as the endless car-and-tire-testing the top professionals use to hone their skills. Although it would be a bold bench racer indeed who claimed Nuvolari, say, was an inferior driver to Senna, on the grounds that the present World Champion was able to practice any time he cared to, losing these "permanent" facilities would be a heavy blow to racing.

And what a tragedy it would be to lose those race-watching pleasures simply not found at present street circuits, like spectacular, high-speed corners in beautiful, park-like surroundings.

Is there danger of losing them? Well, I've watched several famous and useful race tracks go under the plow. Funny, isn't it: Wouldn't you suppose that auto racing, an activity nearing its centennial and one which interests millions of people and which absorbs billions of dollars world-wide, had finally earned a secure place on the planet's surface? But no. While there is still a large number of well-established tracks around, and while against all expectation several new ones have been built in recent years, only a superficial acquaintance with racing history indicates that their survival really twists on the whim of land speculators.

This, I fear, is the hidden danger in the new wave of street circuits. Peculiarities such as the recent high-speed road runs in Mexico and Nevada notwithstanding, I believe the days of long-distance open-road racing are gone forever. But city circuits about two miles around are manageable. They offer an out when a nearby traditional track comes under pressure.

That's why I'd like to see street circuits curbed. Not banned, because they do serve a purpose in certain circumstances. But I feel they should be governed, so they don't threaten the survival of valuable year-round tracks in the neighborhood.

How? Perhaps sanctioning bodies could refuse to authorize a street race in a marketing area already served by a suitable road course or oval. Or, when a conflict must occur, maybe a portion of the profits from the street race could be granted to the nearby permanent track.

And wouldn't it be nice if some of the auto manufacturers, those who are currently getting so much out of their participation in racing, would seed a little money into the sport's training grounds?

Like racing itself, street racing has both good and bad sides. Somehow, the confines of the city seem to bring the sport into sharper focus. Certainly, these "wild in the streets" events are conducted under conditions of the strictest safety and most rigid organization. Yet to many enthusiasts (certainly to me!) the fundamentally outlaw nature of motorsport is a large part of its appeal, and I believe that nowhere is that part so clearly evident as in a race held on ordinary city streets. Many individuals in society need periodic relief from society's regulation, so racing has value as an escape. But most "antidotes to civilization," the ones commonly accepted by polite society, anyway, involve an escape from the confines of the city. Street racing brings the fugitive thing right downtown. Racing's "terrifying anarchy" comes out well in these events. Those black marks on the street carry a special meaning and excitement.

But I would like to see something done to ensure they won't write the entire future of auto racing.

SCCA/Coors Racetruck Challenge

by TOMMY ARCHER

*T*HE SPORTS CAR CLUB OF America's Racetruck Challenge is just that! The season's 11 races were won by five different drivers and four different manufacturers. Jeep won the manufacturers championship by just one point over Nissan. And I managed to squeak the series' heaviest, tallest truck (my Stroh's Jeep Comanche) into the drivers championship by just a three-point margin over Genuine Nissan Parts Nissan driver Jeff Krosnoff. We—my teammate, brother, and third place man in the points, Bobby, and I felt, going into the 1988 season, that it was going to be tough. Boy, were we right on that!

The fields were big and fast. You knew every time you showed up, that just about anybody could be up front. (Bobby's and my patented "Stroh's draft" was often put to good use.) For instance, at every event the top six grid positions—which were then inverted for the start of the race—were fought for by at least 10 trucks. With eight manufacturers involved, the competition was intense with a lot of contact. (There was also some very hard hitting by a few of the over-anxious drivers, some of whom were called in for a chat with "the long arm of the law" [SCCA].) Mike Rutherford won the first race of the season in his Dave Wolin, Inc. Mitsubishi. Ray Kong, fourth in points, captured a win in his Genuine Nissan Parts Nissan. Steve Saleen drove his General Tire/Wards Ford Ranger to one win and fifth in the points battle. And Krosnoff equalled my number of wins—all of which were in street races—with four victories.

By all signs, the 1989 version of the Racetruck Challenge should be one great show with all the major players returning for more bump-drafting fun. See you then!

The Archer brothers' "Stroh's draft" in the Coors Racetruck Challenge was put to good use. Tommy won the series, Bobby was third, and Jeep took the manufacturers title. Photo/Sidell Tilghman.

SCCA/Coors Racetruck Challenge

On the Pocono oval for the first time, the Racetrucks had their share of mishaps. Jeff Krosnoff was tagged from behind, dropped off the course into the infield dirt, then returned to the circuit in 11th place. Krosnoff tied Tommy Archer for season wins, but settled for second only three points down. Photo/Ken Brown-Competition Photographers.

The lead was up for grabs at Sears Point when Bobby Archer (#32) and Ray Kong (#87) tangled. Mike Rutherford slipped by for his only season victory. Photo/Art Flores.

Oops! John Norris lost it at St. Pete and found the tire wall. Mitsubishi placed a distant fourth in their quest for the manufacturers title. Photo/Ken Brown-Competition Photographers.

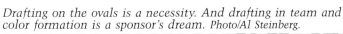

Drafting on the ovals is a necessity. And drafting in team and color formation is a sponsor's dream. Photo/Al Steinberg.

Nissan's artillery in the manufacturers war outnumbered Jeep by three trucks, with Nissan scoring the most wins, but Jeep captured the title by a single point. Photo/Art Flores.

The fastest line out of a corner is over the bumps, as is demonstrated here by Scott Sharp, son of longtime Nissan racer Bob. Scott drove a Dodge Ram-50 to eighth in the series, with a pair of sixths his best. Photo/Sidell Tilghman.

SCCA/Escort Trans-Am

by LAURA CULLEY

AUDI OF AMERICA HIT THE Escort Trans-Am running with an unbeatable combination. Defending champion, Scott Pruett, Darin Brassfield, Willy T. Ribbs, and Paul Gentilozzi, all captured their own champagne bottles, but this was the year of the all-wheel drive Audi Quattro. The manufacturers championship fell to the German juggernaut at Mid-Ohio and Hurley Haywood sewed up the driver's title at Mosport.

Despite some of the closest competition in the 23-year history of the series, the Audi Quattro turbos quietly dominated this year's Escort Trans-Am. Although they looked more like a quarter-acre farm in the paddock, the all-wheel drive feature literally pulled the cumbersome looking cars through the corners and slung them on their way.

But the real "Audi Advantage" came in the capability of the all-wheel drive system to last the entire race. Dubbed early on as the Anteater, the production-chassied Quattros zoomed through track conditions that slowed everyone else to a crawl. Where two-wheel drive cars slipped and slid, Haywood, Stuck and Roehrl pressed on like sure-footed, Alps-bred mountain goats. Add to this automotive edge Hurley Haywood's championship-winning driving philosophy; Hans Stuck's never-leave-an-inch-of-track-unused style; and Walter Roehrl's all-terrain expertise. Combine the above with preparation by Bob Tullius' Group 44 team and a multi-million dollar budget and it was all over but the champagne spraying.

Throughout the year, Haywood happily played tortoise to Stuck and Roehrl's hare.

Le Mans winner and former IMSA champion Hurley Haywood earned his first Trans-Am crown in 1988 in the controversial all-wheel-drive Audi Quattro. Photos/Steve Mohlenkamp.

"I was hired to win the championship," he said matter-of-factly. "I had a very good handle on what was going on around me and beating people that had a chance to beat me in the championship. I would let Hans or Walter go out and be the rabbit, get the guys to race with them and down they went. I was perfectly content to collect as many points as I could and they made my job very easy."

In fact, half of their wins came with the help of the rest of the field. Early in the season, Roush Racing Crew Chief Lee White put it in perspective saying, "They (the Audis) haven't taken anything we didn't give them."

By the time they reached Cleveland, Haywood had two wins and the points lead and the Group 44/Audi of America troops had won four out of six races. Haywood's patience outlasted the competition in Dallas. Then Willy T. Ribbs and Scott Pruett handed the Detroit race over on a silver platter after their last-lap self-destruct move.

"I could have written that in stone," said Haywood. "I could have raced those guys to the end, but I knew Willy and Scott were going to get themselves in trouble. So I just conducted myself so I wouldn't get collected."

European rally champion Walter Roehrl won Niagara Falls ending up in a different time zone from the rest of the lapped field. Then German flying ace Hans Stuck stormed Cleveland, Brainerd, the Meadowlands, and a very wet Mid-Ohio. To cap off the season, Roehrl took the season finale at St. Petersburg, for a total of eight Audi wins.

The Oldsmobile, Chevrolet and Lincoln/Mercury folks were working as hard as they could to cut their own piece of the pie, chasing the all-wheel drive Audis with everything they had.

He never won a race, but Irv Hoerr scored points in 11 of 13 events to earn the runner-up spot in the series, driving an Olds Cutlass. Photo/Stan Clinton.

West German Hans Stuck proved his prowess in the rain by winning the very wet Mid-Ohio contest. Of the eight races he entered, Haywood's Audi teammate won half of them. Photo/Sidell Tilghman.

Paul Gentilozzi snatched the first-ever Escort Trans-Am victory for Oldsmobile at the Long Beach season-opener in May. His win with the Budweiser Oldsmobile Cutlass Supreme was also the first for the big block, 9-to-1 engine. After a third at Detroit and four more top-10 finishes using a combination of V6 and V8 power, Gentilozzi's fortunes see-sawed back to 10th in the overall point standings.

But it was Series newcomer, Irv Hoerr, who chased Haywood's points lead all year with the RA Hoerr Oldsmobile Cutlass Supreme. Unfortunately, he couldn't fit a win in edgewise and ended up second. Running a V6 power plant (with the exception of a low-compression V8 at Road America), Hoerr hoped to capitalize on the lower weight tire wear. Every time out, Hoerr qualified in the Fast Five and made a total of five winner's circle appearances.

Despite some of the closest competition among factory-supported teams in the series' 23-year history, the Audi Quattro turbos quietly dominated this year's Escort Trans-Am. Photo/Jim Hatfield.

Lyn St. James claimed a well-earned third at the season opener, then spent the rest of the year trying to get back onto the victory stand. Photo/Sidell Tilghman.

Lyn St. James.
Photo/Bob Brodbeck.

Although '87 champ Scott Pruett stepped into the winner's circle four times, it was near the end of the season before he grabbed his first win of two. Photo/Sidell Tilghman.

Scott Pruett.
Photo/Taylors Photography.

Paul Gentilozzi scored the first-ever Trans-Am victory for Oldsmobile at the Long Beach opener, then see-sawed back to 10th in the standings. Photo/Sidell Tilghman.

Paul Gentilozzi.
Photo/Art Flores.

After a memorable '87 season, Deborah Gregg's '88 results in a Roush Merkur XR4Ti were less than notable. Her best placing was a fifth at Detroit. Here she leads the Camaro of Jim Derhaag, who was fourth in the standings. *Photo/Art Flores.*

At Mosport, Darin Brassfield passed the crippled Audi of Walter Roehrl to gain his third career Trans-Am victory, his only win of the '88 season. Driving the Pacific Summit/Mobil 1 Corvette, this win and four more top-five finishes were good enough for a fifth in points. *Photo/Art Flores.*

Bruce Nesbitt's Ford Mustang lead's the Chevrolet Beretta of R. K. Smith. *Photo/Art Flores.*

Les Lindley switched between a V6 and a V8 for his Camaro throughout the year, uncertain which he liked best. The high point of his season was not this encounter with the wall but a third at Cleveland. *Photo/Ken Brown-Competition Photographers.*

"We're not disappointed with our performance this year," said Hoerr. "Coming into a new series, we thought we'd be lucky to run in the top five. Then we started out the year on the front row."

The closest was Long Beach. Starting on the outside pole, Hoerr was knocked into the first turn wall at the start. After hurried repairs before the red-flag restart, he started at the back of the pack plus about 15 seconds. By race end, he had won—physically, on the track—the event. Unfortunately, the one-lap penalty received for backing into the pits bumped him back to fifth.

"If I hadn't backed up, I don't believe that I could have run the race," he explained. "The wheel wouldn't turn and I think with the tire being off the rim we would have worn through the wheel and into the rotor and probably not been able to go on before we got around to the pits."

A win was tantalizingly close at Brainerd in a spectacular down-in-the-dirt duel with Stuck until a flat tire knocked him back to fifth in the closing laps.

Scott Pruett's 1988 season was a last-minute addendum to his IMSA GTO effort, and it showed. Additionally, he further split his concentration with Indy

cars. In Trans-Am, the Roush Racing crew started out the season with a 310 V8 engine in the Stroh Light/Ford Authorized Remanufactured Parts Merkur. When it didn't perform quite up to expectations, they made a mid-year switch to a low-compression, 9-to-1 power plant.

Although Pruett stepped into the winner's circle four times with repeated Fast Five appearances, it was Lime Rock before he grabbed his first win. Then he followed up with another flag-to-flag win at Road America to finish third in the series.

Darin Brassfield spent the first part of the season developing on the run. Following a third-place in Dallas and a fourth at Niagara Falls, the 9-to-1 Corvette suffered a variety of niggling mechanical problems, keeping Brassfield out of the championship hunt. But when his Mobile 1/Pacific Summit Corvette hooked up, thanks to the dedicated persistence of Crew Chief Chuck Looper, it had the guts to get after the Audis. He finally snagged his first win from the clutches of Walter Roehrl on Mosport's final lap after an oh-so-close second to Pruett at Lime Rock. Then he put a final second-place stroke to the series picture at the St. Petersburg season finale to take fifth in series points.

A little mix-up at Dallas as Jim Derhaag and Steven Petty stop to exchange names and addresses. Photo/Steve Mohlenkamp.

Darin Brassfield's Corvette is reflected in its highly-polished wheel. Photo/Randy McKee.

Les Lindley switched color schemes on his Camaro for Detroit to become the "Spirit of Detroit." Willy T. Ribbs drove Lindley's second trademark-yellow Chevy. Photos/Jim Hatfield, Steve Mohlenkamp (inset).

European rally ace Walter Roehrl made six appearances for Audi, winning twice. Photo/Steve Mohlenkamp.

Minnesota's Jim Derhaag performed his darndest for the hometown crowd at Brainerd, finishing third, his best for the year. Photo/Art Flores.

From Peoria, Illinois, season runner-up Irv Hoerr. Photo/Taylors Photography.

If you're looking for a good show, who do you call? Willy T. Ribbs, of course. Willy drove seven races in Les Lindley's Camaro, putting some crinkles on its roof when he won at Sears Point. Photo/Art Flores.

Jerry Clinton's best was a pair of 10ths in an Olds. Photo/Taylors Photography.

Driving one of Hoerr's Oldsmobiles, Mike Ciasulli was named Rookie of the Year. Photo/Taylors Photography.

His Nissan 300ZX was the fastest at Long Beach, but Paul Newman's season was a dismal one. Crashes and the car's lack of reliability put him out more than once. Photo/Steve Mohlenkamp.

Soft-spoken Les Lindley was eighth in points. Photo/Taylors Photography.

Although he only took one pole, Hans Stuck scored two fastest laps and four wins. Photo/Steve Mohlenkamp.

Thirteenth for the year was the best Deborah Gregg could do. Photo/Steve Mohlenkamp.

Darin Brassfield's dad, Jerry (r), co-drove a Camaro with his son at Dallas to a remarkable third place. Darin teamed up with Jerry when his Corvette fizzled on the pace lap. Photo/Taylors Photography.

Hospitality area umbrellas create a vision of symmetry. Photo/Steve Mohlenkamp.

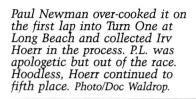

Paul Newman over-cooked it on the first lap into Turn One at Long Beach and collected Irv Hoerr in the process. P.L. was apologetic but out of the race. Hoodless, Hoerr continued to fifth place. Photo/Doc Waldrop.

A very surprised yet happy trio at Long Beach. Paul Gentilozzi didn't believe he'd won, Hurley Haywood only thought he was second, and Lyn St. James first had to be found before she could celebrate her third. Photo/Bruce R. Schulman.

Instead of the usual tube-frame, replica-bodied, rear-drive Trans-Am entry, Audi campaigned an all-wheel-drive Audi 200 Turbo Quattro equipped with a turbocharged 5-cylinder engine. The car, while modified for competition, was based on the same car available to the public. Photo/Courtesy of Audi.

Dubbed early on as the Anteater, the production-chassied Audi Quattros zoomed through track conditions that slowed everyone else to a crawl. Combine this with preparation by Bob Tullius' (with headset) Group 44 team and a multi-million dollar budget and you're bound to win both the drivers and manufacturers championships. Photos/Michael Dunn, Barry Tenin (inset).

Always exciting Willy T. Ribbs took a down-to-the-last-turn win at Sears Point in Les Lindley's F.S.I. Camaro. But it was his third-place finish at Road America which elevated him into the top spot in the all-time Escort Trans-Am career earnings list. With that drive, he had wheeled the TA "door slammer" to a total of $286,783 in winnings.

Series Technical Administrator, Dave Watson, did his best to keep a level playing field. At Cleveland, Watson slapped 100 pounds and a 54mm restrictor on "Audi's Advantage." A Trans-Am Owner's Advisory Committee was formed at Brainerd which suggested even more adjustments were required. Watson agreed, adding another 100 pounds and reducing the Audi tire contact patch by one-half inch. However, with Goodyear on their side, the Audi tire size was restored at Mosport.

Lots of other designs were adjusted, too. Irv Hoerr lost half the weight break in the five-out-of-six stock component rule plus another 50-pound V6 penalty before he led a lap. The 9-to-1 contingent also gained weight during the season.

Brainerd turned out to be Jim Derhaag's finest hour. Earning his first and only Fast Five qualifying spot, Derhaag scored a third-place finish, bringing his Sign Art Camaro out for the winner's circle festivities on his home track. With a total of 11 out of 13 top-10 finishes, Derhaag finished fourth in the Series points battle, the highest posting for the 310 V8 crowd.

Lyn St. James claimed a well-earned third at the season opener at Long Beach, then spent the remainder of the season trying to catch back up to the victory stand. After narrowly missing it twice, St. James scored her first Fast Five spot at Lime Rock with the Secret-sponsored Merkur XR4Ti. During the year, she never finished lower than 11th with a total of nine top-10 finishes to take seventh in the overall championship and the best consistency rating of the entire field.

Les Lindley switched between V6s and V8s throughout the year, uncertain which he liked best. His high season mark was a third at Cleveland, with fourths at Long Beach, Sears Point and Mosport.

But no one tried harder than Chris Kneifel. Deserting the Olivetti/Bruce Jenner Racing Porsche 944 early on for the "less evil" V8 Pontiac Trans-Am, Kneifel was constantly thwarted no matter what he did. Working with a brand new crew that never really came together, Kneifel—even when he started last—repeatedly clawed his way to within spitting distance of solid a top-five finish, only to break. The real heartbreaker was Cleveland. Sitting comfortably in second, Kneifel pitted on the last lap, his gauges pegged. He limped around one more time to take his season-best sixth place. Kneifel's effort was recognized with the 1988 Hard Charger award.

Mike Ciasulli (RA Hoerr Oldsmobile Cutlass Supreme) was named the Escort Trans-Am Rookie of the Year. The Lindley Racing crew, led by Pat McFall, was recognized as the series Crew of the Year. And a Special Appreciation award went to Baja Boats boss, Doug Smith.

Jack Baldwin ran two races in the Morrison-Cook Corvette, scoring a second at Mid-Ohio and a seventh at Road America. Photo/Art Flores.

Paul Newman's best finish was a seventh at his home track, Lime Rock Park. Photo/Steve Mohlenkamp.

The Meadowlands race saw some good dicing among Deborah Gregg (#3), Mike Ciasulli (#16) and Chris Kneifel (#72). Photo/Tony Mezzacca.

The Audi 200 Quattro: The 1988 SCCA Trans-Am Series Champion.

Last April, Audi joined the Trans-Am circuit. Against all odds. And against all tradition.

After all, this premier road racing event is normally the province of powerful behemoths—specially built, "tube frame" race cars whose resemblance to production cars is merely skin deep.

But Audi had a more practical agenda: to prove that the same permanent all-wheel drive Quattro technology found in *our* street cars could beat *their* race cars.

So we entered a team of new Audi 200 Quattros. Yes, *four-door sedans*. Complete with power steering and a five-cylinder engine which—though admittedly modified—produced about 100 bhp less than most of the competition.

No matter. Because Audi quickly proved the old definition of performance no longer applies. Now, it's brainpower versus horsepower. And our highly evolved Quattro system outperforms by outsmarting—with a differential that assigns power to the wheels that need it most. As traction and cornering conditions dictate.

Soon, an awesome string of victories was compiled. Including six of the first nine SCCA Trans-Am races.

In fact, as Quattro's dominance over the field became self-evident, some midseason handicaps were

Audi Started The Sea
And Finished It

NHRA-IHRA/Drag Racing

by PHIL R. ELLIOTT

*I*T WAS AN INTERESTING, entertaining year for the acceleration sport which pits men and machines against both each other and timing lights 1320 feet apart. After almost 17 years, the five-second barrier was broken; a barrier with the same mystique as the once seemingly unachievable four-minute mile. From that moment Mike Snively rocketed to the very first "five" until the instant that Eddie Hill recorded the historic first "four," nearly two decades had passed—two decades to advance one full second. But this achievement was over-shadowed by an even bigger story.

In September of 1987, Billy Meyer occupied an enviable position in drag racing. His race car was heavily sponsored and highly competitive. But more importantly, he had built a state-of-the-art drag strip a few miles from Dallas that was a racer's dream-come-true. And the fans showed up in droves to experience this latest jewel in the National Hot Rod Association's (NHRA) crown.

One year later, Billy still owned his famous Texas MotorPlex with its fabulous creature comforts and stunning performances. And he had added to his portfolio the International Hot Rod Association (IHRA)—with a balance sheet colored mostly in red and a just-ended season colored mostly in rain. To add to his gut-wrenching year, ownership of the IHRA has seemed synonymous with hassles legal in nature. He has been involved in lawsuits, countersuits and business suits far more than firesuits throughout the '88 season.

A suit and countersuit with/against the NHRA over the Texas MotorPlex and their several-year contract was mutually ended, with both sides claiming victory in press releases.

Additional law suits were the end result when a season-long dispute involving the Pro Stock contingent came to a head in Milan, Michigan during the Motorcraft Northern Nationals. There, following qualifying, the top two qualifiers—Bob Glidden's Motorcraft Ford and the Reher and Morrison Chevy—pulled out because of "unfair and inconsistent" treatment . . . or were thrown out. It all depended on which story you listened to. Simultaneously, as the teams were stating they would never attend another IHRA event, the IHRA was banning the two entries from any further IHRA competition in 1988. The end result was more law suits against the IHRA requesting, in Glidden's case, compensation of $30,000,000!

Legal confrontations not withstanding, the more traditional confrontations also took place at drag strips across the country.

On the strength of four wins, in 1988 Joe Amato, here with wife Jere, secured his second NHRA Top Fuel championship. He also won the IHRA's Budweiser Spring Nationals and the Angus Nitro Showdown.
Photo/Leslie Lovett.

Smoke swirled off his tires as 1988 NHRA World Champion Joe Amato performed a burnout with his TRW-backed dragster. Interestingly, the same basic Goodyear tires have been used for the past 10 years in drag racing. Amato's crewman, Dick Moore, displayed his unequivocal pride in his main man on the back of his tee shirt! Photos/Jim Phillipson, Taylors Photography (inset).

Photo/Jim Phillipson.

A crewman's work is never done. Photo/Leslie Lovett.

Ercie Hill, Eddie Hill's wife and favorite team sidekick, returned the record-setting dragster after Eddie became the top qualifier with an ET of 5.082, 279.24 MPH, at the NHRA U.S. Nationals. Hill had a dynamite season! Photo/Ron McQueeney.

Eddie Hill made drag racing history during the IHRA Texas Nationals on April 9 by becoming the first driver to crack the five-second barrier for a quarter-mile run. Not only was Hill's 4.99-second run the quickest of all time, but his speed through the traps at the end of the run, 288.55 MPH, was also the fastest ever recorded. Then, in October, at the Fram Supernationals in Houston, he was clocked at 4.93 but couldn't back it up per the NHRA's one percent rule. An ET of 4.99 was backed up, however, and Eddie Hill went into the record books as the NHRA national record holder as well. Photos/Doc Waldrop (bottom), Leslie Lovett (right).

Lori Johns made her Top Fuel racing debut in 1988, becoming one of the 10 quickest ever in just three months! Photo/Taylors Photography.

Tim Ferrel, left, coaches Lori Johns. Her best effort at the end of the season was a 5.09. Photo/Leslie Lovett.

TOP FUEL

The actual racing season dawned in Phoenix, as many of the pros showed their newest rides during the annual NHRA booked-in event at Charlie Allen's desert facility. The '88 season began exactly the same way '87 had ended: Dick LaHaie won.

The show moved on to Pomona's NHRA Chief Auto Parts Winternationals where, again, Dick LaHaie won, defeating Joe Amato. LaHaie even set low ET in the final round, giving him the appearance of the the man to beat for yet another season. He went on to the NHRA Motorcraft Gatornationals at Gainesville and sat on the pole. He then seemed to almost disappear from the sport. In spite of staging his normal strong, competitive efforts, he was overshadowed and out-performed by several other drivers.

While LaHaie was winning, a discrepancy over rear wheel size had given Eddie Hill most of the Top Fuel ink in California. Continuing on to Florida, Hill constantly overpowerd the race track so that he was ninth after qualifying—directly opposite LaHaie on the ladder. Hill found the combination in Round One, however, easily defeating LaHaie with a 5.08, which he later backed up with a 5.06 and a new NHRA record. He went on to win the race, his first national event.

Darrell Gwynn and Gene Snow won the first two IHRA events (rain-delayed Super Nationals, Bradenton, Florida; Winter Nationals, Darlington, South Carolina). Next, the invited Pros headed for Meyer's MotorPlex and the Texas Nationals. It was there, in front of a relatively sparse crowd, that history was made.

On April 9, 1988, during qualifying for the Texas Nationals, Eddie Hill seared the record books with an ET of 4.99 (288.55 MPH). A veteran of drag racing, motorcycle racing and drag boats, the 52-year-old Hill had reentered the asphalt wars in 1986. During his reacquaintance years, he was anything but competitive. But with a new 300-inch wheelbase car and sponsors (Super Shops and Pennzoil), he suddenly found himself holding both national records under both sanctions and one of those was in the mythical fours.

The actual race had to wait a week because rain again hit, but Hill came back to win. He continued his streak, again winning the NHRA's A.C. Delco Southern Nationals in Atlanta.

Eddie Hill studies the numbers which helped him break the records. He learned, no doubt, that a quarter mile equals the length of four-plus football fields, within which distance a Top Fueler is now capable of accelerating to more than five times the legal speed limit...in less than the time it takes the average family car to reach 30 MPH! Photo/Leslie Lovett.

"Big Daddy" Don Garlits raced his first dragster, the vintage "Swamp Rat #1," at the Bakersfield Fuel & Gas Championship in '88, thirty years after he did it the first time. Photo/Jim Phillipson.

Flames shot skyward from the hot Top Fuel engines as Darrell Gwynn took off to set a national ET record of 5.05 at the Performance SeaFair Nationals in Seattle against Connie Kalitta. Gwynn won six times, two more than Amato, but was only second in points. Photo/Jim Phillipson.

Photo/Leslie Lovett.

Funny Car star Kenny Bernstein didn't win his fourth NHRA Funny Car championship until the last two rounds of the final race at Pomona! He became the second Funny Car driver to post a time under 5.30 seconds at the Winston Finals with a 5.295 elapsed time on his last pass. Photo/Taylors Photography.

Ed McCulloch, in the Miller High Life Oldsmobile Cutlass Supreme, grabbed a record six national event championships on his way to winning the IHRA title— his first series crown. He also won two NHRA events. Photo/Doc Waldrop.

Pit crews come in all sorts of packages. Harry Scribner's comes in pink. This could only happen in California, where Scribner took the Pro Stock victory over Don Beverly at the NHRA's Motorcraft California Nationals. Photo/Tyler Photo Illustrators.

Gene Snow won the next event, the IHRA's Pro Am Nationals at Rockingham, North Carolina. The show moved on to Memphis and the NHRA Quaker State Mid South Nationals, won by Darrell Gwynn. Joe Amato finally made it back into victory circle, taking the IHRA Spring Nationals at Bristol, Tennessee. Darrell Gwynn again found the winning combination, overcoming the field at the NHRA K-Mart/Champion Cajun Nationals in Baton Rouge. Gene Snow put together the next consecutive wins, with victories at the IHRA Summer Nationals in Atco, New Jersey and Atlanta's NHRA Winston All-Stars. Darrell Gwynn came back the next weekend to win the NHRA Budweiser Springnationals in Columbus, Ohio. But then Gene Snow replied with two more consecutive wins: the IHRA Northern Nationals in Milan, Michigan and the NHRA Molson Le Grandnational in Montreal, Quebec.

Then Joe Amato once more made his presence felt, winning the NHRA Budweiser Summernationals in Englishtown, New Jersey. The troupe headed westward for the new NHRA "left coast" events. At the Sears Point (near San Francisco) Motorcraft California Nationals, Amato won again, over a stout LaHaie. But Gwynn, rebounding at the Performance Corner SeaFair Nationals in Seattle the following week, set a new NHRA record (5.05) in the process of winning.

Two weeks later, Amato answered Gwynn by beating him at the NHRA Quaker State Northstar Nationals in Brainerd, Minnesota. This was followed by Gene Snow reminding the world he was still around, by taking the IHRA World Nationals in Norwalk, Ohio.

In Indianapolis the next weekend at the NHRA U.S. Nationals, Amato reacted by beating Snow—in spite of Snow's having posted a powerful 5.006. Amato was undoubtedly aided by the fact the Snow's throttle linkage fell off in the final round. "For want of a nickel part . . ."

The next event, the IHRA U.S. Open Nationals, was won by Paul Smith. Then Darrell Gwynn picked up his fifth victory of the year, winning the NHRA Castrol GTX Keystone Nationals in Reading, Pennsylvania. Eddie Hill came back to the victory stand with his 5.110 run at the IHRA Fall Nationals in Bristol. Then all eyes were upon Texas.

Billy Meyer and his IHRA continued to be plagued by bad weather, rain postponing his Chief Auto Parts Nationals. But while Dallas was inundated, the wet stuff barely watered Houston Raceway Park's newly placed sod lawns. The contrast typified the season-long luck of the IHRA versus the NHRA.

Gene Snow was the first to go into the "fours" at Houston's NHRA Supernationals. His 4.997 led qualifying. At the other end of the spectrum was Eddie Hill, who blew everything in his trailer and actually announced over the P.A. that he was folding up his tent. The fellowship of racing bloomed, however, and many of his competitors rushed to his aid—probably to their regret. Hill ended up hitting 5.03, 5.04, 5.05, 4.99, and 4.93 to win the Top Fuel race over Joe Amato, who ran a superb 5.00 (287.35 MPH).

Back at the MotorPlex, the weather around Dallas finally shaped up for the IHRA. Eddie Hill took the Top Fuel win over Darrell Gwynn. Eddie and Gene both ran "fours" and were joined in the twilight zone by unheralded Richard Holcomb, who used lots of Clayton Harris horsepower and an eight-year-old chassis to run a 4.99. Connie Kalitta, who had run some 5.0s since installing a direct drive unit, hit a whopping 287.08 MPH for top speed. The race ended the IHRA season—a season in which eight of the scheduled 11 races were hampered by rain. Gene Snow was awarded the IHRA Top Fuel championship, a crown he unequivocally claimed back in July.

Holder of the top speed record of 286.71, which he set at the Gatornationals in March, Top Fueler Frank Bradley checks the hydrometer to balance out the tune-up between the air/fuel mix. Photo/Leslie Lovett.

Love blooms on the dragstrip. Shirley Muldowney and her longtime crew chief Tahn Tabler were wed on St. Valentine's Day. Photo/Leslie Lovett.

Gene Snow, a 50-year-old native of Ft. Worth, Texas, won five IHRA races en route to his second straight Top Fuel championship. On the NHRA tour, the "Snowman" won twice and was the first driver to break the five-second mark in the NHRA. He held the record at 4.996 until Eddie Hill smashed it with an ET of 4.990. Photo/Taylors Photography.

Lori Johns is fast becoming a super star in Top Fuel racing. She qualified in the top five at a number of events. The 1988 season saw the fastest qualifying fields in Top Fuel history. Photo/Taylors Photography.

Driving a two-year-old ex-Amato dragster whose aerodynamic design the NHRA troops rejected as dangerous when Don Garlits flipped in a similar vehicle, Butch Blair is still looking for his first win. Perhaps questioning his choice to stay with the car and the series, he calls it, "Blair's Fugowie." Photo/Leslie Lovett.

Johnny West, of Chandler, Arizona, never reached the finals in the NHRA. He was, nonetheless, eighth in the Funny Car standings.
Photo/Leslie Lovett.

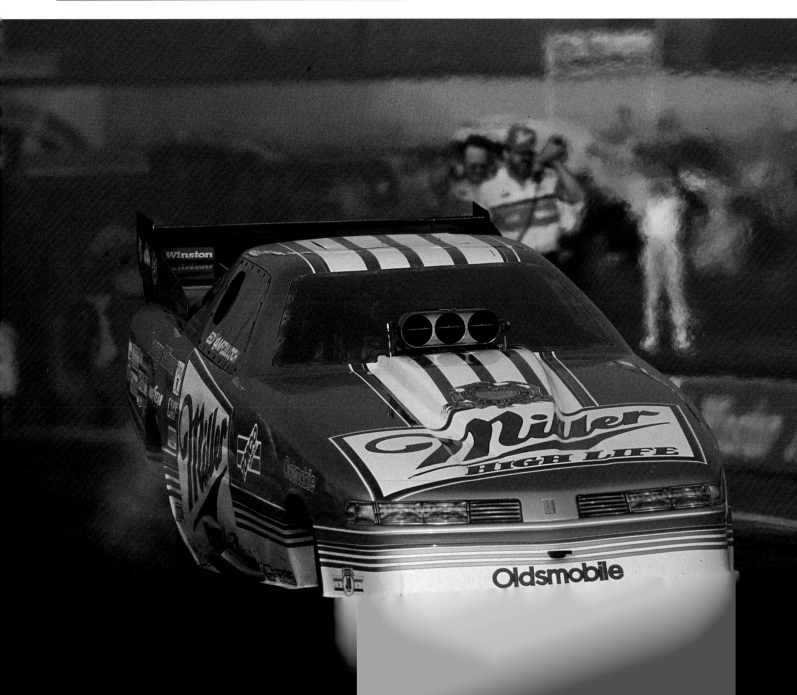

Hemet, California's Ed McCulloch decimated the IHRA competition from the first race in July through the end of the season. He also won the prestigious NHRA U.S. Nationals and the AC Delco Southern Nationals to place fifth in the NHRA Funny Car points.
Photo/Taylors Photography.

Putting in his bid for the title, Don Prudhomme took two consecutive wins at the Molson Le Grandnational and the Summernationals. Although Bernstein won at Seattle's new strip, SeaFair, it was Prudhomme who set the record with an ET of 5.30.
Photo/Leslie Lovett.

Don Prudhomme's total of 37 national event wins is second only to Bob Glidden's. Photo/Taylors Photography.

Four-time IHRA World Champion Mark Oswald, the only driver to win series championships on both tours in the same season, ended 1988 as the runner-up in both series. He and crew chief Leonard Hughes put the finishing touches on a tune-up. Photo/Leslie Lovett.

Despite evidence to the contrary, like the tire print across crewman Jim Male's chest, Kenny Bernstein didn't really run him over at NorthStar. Photo/Leslie Lovett.

FUNNY CAR

The bodied nitro-burners were every bit as exciting as their dragster brothers during '88. For the most part, the dominating forces in Funny Car competition were Ed McCulloch, Mark Oswald, Kenny Bernstein and John Force.

But it was Dale Pulde who shocked everyone at the NHRA season-opener, winning the Winternationals convincingly in Bill Schultz' Oldsmobile. Then the expected returned with Bernstein putting together a string of 5.3s to overwhelm the field at the Gatornationals; Ed McCulloch winning the Southern Nationals; and Mark Oswald taking the inaugural Funny Car crown at Memphis' Mid South Nationals.

Consistent performances and six visits to the title round with three victories helped Kenny Bernstein, in the Budweiser King, take his fourth-in-a-row NHRA Funny Car World title. Photo/Taylors Photography.

In a freak accident at the NorthStar event, Bernstein was unable to get his car in reverse. While the crew was giving him a hand, the car made a sudden move forward, scattering the crew and scaring everyone else. Luckily, no one was hurt. Photo/Phil Burgess.

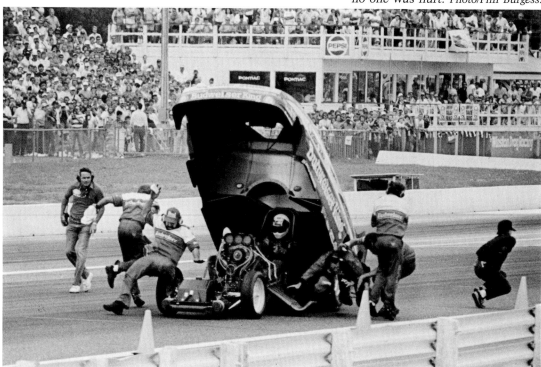

By this point in the season, the middle of May, the IHRA had run five events. Mark Oswald won the first event scheduled, the Super Nationals. Tripp Shumake took the Winter Nationals at Darlington. Ed McCulloch then proceeded with back-to-back victories in the Texas Nationals (with an ET of 5.25) and the Pro-Am Nationals. Mark Oswald re-entered the picture, winning Bristol's Spring Nationals.

Two wizards of Funny Car tuners: left, million-dollar wrench for Kenny Bernstein, Dale Armstrong; and Austin Coil, who tuned John Force to a third-place NHRA finish. Photo/Leslie Lovett.

Clutch timers are definitely in drag racing's future, with speeds of close to 300 MPH predicted by the end of 1989 because of their use. But when they fail, look out! Shirley Muldowney just barely avoided disaster in Houston when a clutch timer failure blew the heads off the engine and created a fireball. Photo/Leslie Lovett.

A blower exploded and Sherm Gunn found himself in an air-conditioned Funny Car when the body flew off. Photo/Taylors Photography.

Drag racing draws thousands of race fans on a weekend to watch action like this burnout by Mike Dunn in his Pisano Olds Cutlass. Average weekend attendance at NHRA events was nearly 77,000 in '88, while the IHRA saw a 41 percent increase to over 47,000. Dunn came out on top in two finals and set six top speeds, ending up seventh in the NHRA season points. Photo/Doc Waldrop.

Kyle, son of Top Fuel racer Bill Mullins, spent most of the summer in the pits playing with his favorite toy, the Monster Slick.
Photo/Leslie Lovett.

After two decades of trying, Bruce Larson found the way to not one but two winner's circles. He topped the field at both the sixth event on the IHRA calendar—the Summer Nationals—and the fifth event on the NHRA schedule—the K-Mart/Champion Cajun Nationals. Mark Oswald won the the next NHRA show, the Winston All-Stars and the NHRA points were so tight that no driver could be considered a favorite. To make matters more interesting, the next NHRA event, the Budweiser Spring Nationals, was won by John Force. And then Don Prudhomme put in his bid with two consecutive wins at Le Grandnational and the Summernationals. The four "usuals" took the next four events: Oswald, the Motorcraft California Nationals; Bernstein, the Performance Corner SeaFair Nationals; Force, the Quaker State Northstar Nationals. Although it was Bernstein who won at SeaFair, it was Prudhomme who set the new strip's record with an ET of 5.30.

Third in the NHRA Funny Car standings, John Force posted wins at the Budweiser Springnationals, Quaker State NorthStar Nationals and Winston Finals.
Photo/Taylors Photography.

At the Molson Le Grandnational in Montreal, John Force was number-one qualifier; set the best time of the event; and rounded off the day with the event's top speed. But is was Don Prudhomme who emerged the winner.
Photo/Leslie Lovett.

Four years of experimentation with the unique Australian McGee motor and ex-World Champion Gary Beck continues pushing forward with its development. Created specifically for drag racing by Phil and Chris McGee, it's a double overhead cam power plant. Kenny Bernstein has jumped on the bandwagon by offering Beck the expertise of his crew chief Dale Armstrong to help. Many insiders believe that the future of drag racing just might be inside this motor. Photo/Jim Phillipson.

Al Hanna's Eastern Raider Jet Funny Car lights up the moonlit sky at the Budweiser Summernationals in Englishtown, New Jersey. These cars are strictly for the crowd's entertainment and aren't timed, but speeds are estimated to be around the 250 MPH mark. Photo/Leslie Lovett.

Eric Reed pops his 'chutes at the end of his run at Sears Point.
Photo/Jim Phillipson.

The "Chevy of the Year" was in the hands of Tony Christian, who took this Beretta to a third in NHRA Pro Stock points. Christian made it into the finals three times, winning twice. Photo/Ron McQueeney.

Back in the IHRA, Ed McCulloch decimated the competition from the first race in July through the end of the season. McCulloch opened July with a win at the Northern Nationals and followed it with victory at the World Nationals. His string was interrupted by Dale Pulde who won the U.S. Open Nationals. But McCulloch answered by winning the Fall Nationals, the season finale Chief Auto Parts Nationals and, ultimately, the IHRA World Championship.

The NHRA points battle wasn't so easily decided. After the U.S. Nationals at Indy, also won by McCulloch, the top three in NHRA Funny Car points—Bernstein, Oswald and Force—were separated by only 500 points with Prudhomme lurking in fourth. Bernstein won the next event, the Castrol GTX Keystone Nationals and Oswald won the Big Bud Shootout. However, Mike Dunn won the next two shows, the FRAM Supernationals and the Castrol GTX Fallnationals, both times beating final round opponents who were out of the top half of the points chase.

With less than 100 points separating them going into the last race of the season, Kenny Bernstein and Mark Oswald each was determined to go farther than the other at the Winston Finals. Both qualified well. Both advanced past Round One. But trivia buffs will remember Tom Hoover as the man who, in Round Two, spoiled Mark Oswald's championship chances. While qualifying, Bernstein became the second man to post a Funny Car ET in the 5.2s (5.29), but it was John Force who won this particular battle. The war, however, was indeed won by Bernstein as he captured his unprecedented fourth consecutive NHRA Winston World Championship.

Crawling from the remains of his racer is Steve Hodkinson who blew the blower and body off his ride at the Supernationals. Photo/Leslie Lovett.

PRO STOCK

The story of 1988 Pro Stock can be summarized quickly by mentioning two names: Bob Glidden and Rickie Smith. No, they didn't win every race. In fact, for the first time in Pro Stock history underdogs won races. There were more new names in the winners circle during '88 than in any other season since the inception of the class for "Detroit Hot Rods" back in 1970. Those new faces—none of which were newcomers, just non-winners—included Tony Christian, Morris Johnson, Jr., Harry Scribner, and Jerry Eckman.

With the new IHRA Pro Stock rules similar to those of the NHRA, more cross-overs occurred. Among the beneficiaries of the new status was Warren Johnson who won two NHRA races and, after several years absence from the arena, three IHRA events.

With the 11 IHRA Pro Stock victories being divided among five drivers and the 17 NHRA wins being shared among eight contenders, the two sanctioning bodies were seemingly evenly matched in terms of competitiveness.

The 1988 NHRA Pro Stock World Champion, again and again, Bob Glidden. Photo/Leslie Lovett.

Nine-time NHRA Winston Pro Stock World Champion Bob Glidden owns the NHRA record for most national event wins, 67; most points in a single season, 16,035; and most consecutive wins, nine. He's had more victorious rounds and more appearances in the finals than anyone in NHRA history. This year he set the NHRA ET national record of 7.177, which was added to his all-time top-speed record of 191.32 MPH set in '87. Glidden also set a new IHRA record this year, 7.303-seconds elapsed time, and holds the IHRA record for the most number of event wins. Whew! Photo/Taylors Photography.

Every year over *four* million people visit our research facilities.

At TRW, engineers work on advanced engine and chassis parts with an audience of over four million people. After rigorous lab testing, new ideas are put to the test in grueling NHRA, IMSA and NASCAR competition. Trackside research helps us design better components that stand up to the toughest everyday use.

As part of our "Weekend Research" program, TRW sponsors the Amato Racing team of Top Fuel driver Joe Amato and Top Alcohol Dragster driver Bill Walsh, plus the NHRA Sportsman All-Stars, Grand 9.90 and 900

Club competition. In addition, we support NASCAR and IMSA racing with the Mechanic of the Year Awards and a variety of contingency programs.

When performance is important, ask for TRW engine and chassis parts. TRW Automotive Aftermarket Division, 8001 East Pleasant Valley Road, Cleveland, OH 44131-5582.

At TRW, quality is just the beginning.

TRW Automotive Products

The IHRA victors were: Rickie Smith, the Super Nationals, Winter Nationals, Pro-Am Nationals, and the Northern Nationals; Bob Glidden, the Texas Nationals and the Summer Nationals; Warren Johnson, the Spring Nationals, the Fall Nationals and the Chief Auto Parts Nationals; Harry Scribner, the World Nationals; and Morris Johnson, Jr., the U.S. Open Nationals. Smith's four wins and three runner-up finishes captured the IHRA World Championship by a large margin.

The NHRA winners were: Butch Leal, Chief Auto Parts Winternationals; Bruce Allen, the Motorcraft Gatornationals and the K-Mart/Champion Cajun Nationals; Warren Johnson, the A.C. Delco Southern Nationals and the Winston Finals; Tony Christian, the Quaker State Mid South Nationals and the Quaker State Northstar Nationals; Jerry Eckman, the Winston All-Stars; Bob Glidden, the Budweiser Springnationals, Budweiser Summernationals, Performance Corner SeaFair Nationals, U.S. Nationals, Castrol GTX Keystone Nationals, FRAM Supernationals, Castrol GTX Fallnationals, and the bonus Mr. Gasket Pro Stock Challenge; Morris Johnson, Jr., Molson Le Grandnational; and Harry Scribner, the Motorcraft California Nationals. Bob Glidden's strong season, in which he brought the NHRA record down to 7.27, won him his ninth NHRA Winston World Championship.

Rickie Smith always finds the time to sign an autograph. That's probably why he has lots of fans. Photo/Francis C. Butler.

Rickie Smith, the 1988 IHRA Pro Stock champion, gets his wheels up at Maryland International Raceway on his way to a victory, one of four for the year. Photo/Francis C. Butler.

Scott Geoffrion, driver of the Ken Koretsky Pro Stocker, gets a last good-luck kiss blown his way from girlfriend Bo. Photo/Leslie Lovett.

"Bubba" is what Rickie Smith calls the motor that helped earn him his fourth title in IHRA Pro Stock. Photo/Francis C. Butler.

" With the new IHRA Pro Stock rules similar to those of the NHRA, more cross-overs occurred. Among the beneficiaries of the new status was Warren Johnson who won two NHRA races and, after several years' absence from the arena, three IHRA events. Johnson was number two in NHRA points behind Glidden." Photo/Leslie Lovett.

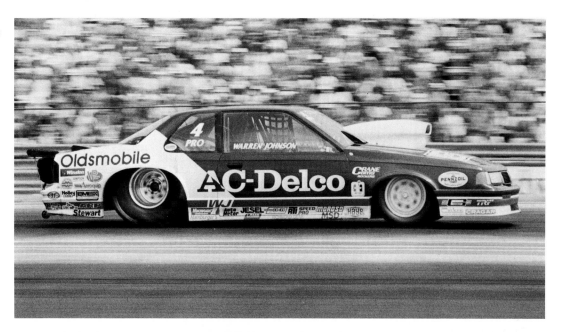

Bruce Allen, driving the Reher & Morrison Chevy Beretta, was fourth in the NHRA Pro Stock season standings, making it into the finals three times and winning twice, at the Gatornationals and the Cajun Nationals. Photo/Doc Waldrop.

From Berwyn, Pennsylvania, "EZ Wider" Chevy Beretta driver Joe Lepone, Jr. never saw the victory lane, but squeaked into ninth in NHRA Pro Stock points by a hair over Mark Pawuk. Photo/Taylors Photography.

Once a year a celebrity race is held at Pomona. Wally and The Beaver (also known as Tony Dow and Jerry Mathers) gave it a go, but only after some tutoring by Professor Frank Hawley, of course. Photo/Leslie Lovett.

With the politics, the "fours" and the races covered, it should be noted that the increase in performance can be attributed to the "three Cs": computers, concrete and clutches. All are technically intertwined so that one cannot get along without the others. Computer readouts showed that clutches slipped the entire track, effectively slowing the cars in exactly the same way that slipping tires do. Smart mechanics began to design and utilize mechanical overrides to force the clutch to hook up solidly. The clutch companies helped with timed "lock-ups," then the smart teams began to try multiple "lock-ups," a sort of mechanical torque converter which constantly changes tightness. With a concrete starting line and asphalt further down the track, tire slippage was encountered at the transition. Texas MotorPlex was built with the entire surface made of concrete, pre-stressed with cables to rid it of expansion joints. While the starting line was not better than any other concrete starting line, the better down-track adhesion enabled fuel cars to pick up performance in both ET and speed. The new Houston track has 1000 feet of concrete, nearly the full length of the timed surface. Seattle extended its concrete pad to 300 feet, plus it is surrounded by oxygen-producing trees. The story is much the same at Maple Grove and both tracks produce outstanding times.

As tracks begin to catch up with the 4,000 horsepower, nitromethane-burning, computer-helped, 500 cubic inch engines, future Elapsed Times will only decrease. They will continue to improve race to race, year to year, until the ferocity of drag race acceleration is limited only by the human frailty of the driver.

Drag racing got three new race tracks in
'88. One was a makeover of Atlanta
Raceway; and the new Memphis facility
hosted its first big-league event in May.
But the best by far was the new track in
Houston, which saw the quickest run
ever in drag racing, when Eddie Hill was
clocked at 4.936! Next year, two more
tracks, the made-over Denver facility, and
the brand-new Topeka Raceway will be
added. Drag racing has made tremendous
strides within the past 10 years or so,
both in terms of ever-increasing
performance and in improving amenities
for competitors and spectators alike.
Photo/Leslie Lovett.

Super Modifieds

Former ISMA title-holder and Oswego track champ Steve Gioia, Jr. (#9) holds off Jerry O'Niel at Thompson. Gioia was fourth for the year in ISMA. Photo/Howard Hodge.

Although he's won the Oswego Budweiser International Classic three times, Eddie Bellinger didn't win his first Oswego track championship until 1988. He and his dad are the only father-and-son team to have ever won track championships at Oswego Speedway. Photo/Howard Hodge.

ISMA champ and former Indy 500 racer Bentley Warren leads Tim Nelson and Joe Gosek at Thompson. While ex-ISMA champ Gosek has over 20 career feature wins, Nelson is a Super Modified up-and-comer. Photo/Howard Hodge.

The International Super Modified Association (ISMA) champion for 1988, Bentley Warren. *Photo/Howard Hodge.*

According to his fans and followers, Eddie Bellinger, in Mike Mazur's *Miller High Life Special*, has, "driven everything and won everything in the Northeast." *Photo/Howard Hodge.*

Wingless, Gene Lee Gibson set a new record of 127+ MPH in his Super Modified in an open-competition race at Salem Speedway in October. *Photo/Larry Van Sickle.*

In the Evans Memorial at Oswego, Dave McKnight, Jr. (#6) managed to stay ahead of Mike Brubaker (#19) and Mike Muldoon (#10). McKnight, one of the top runners from Canada, built his own car and finished in the top 10 in both ISMA and Oswego points. Muldoon took over from A. J. Michaels (who moved into another ride) at the Evans Memorial, then won his first ever feature, the "Y94 FM $10,000 To Win" event. *Photo/Howard Hodge.*

Modifieds

by **MIKE ROWELL**

*I*N THE VERY FIRST RACE OF THE modified season at Orange County Speedway in Rougemont, North Carolina, Reggie Ruggiero won and Mike "Magic Shoes" McLaughlin placed second. For the next 30 races these two would battle for the Modified Tour championship. In the second race at Martinsville, Virginia, McLaughlin won the race and took the points lead which he would hold for the next six months.

"Magic Shoes" lived up to his name this year driving Clyde McLeod's #12. In the first eight races, he had two wins, three seconds and never placed lower than fifth. By the Tour's end, McLaughlin won five races in all. It was not easy to be consistently fast since the team's sponsor dropped out early in the season and did not come back until August.

The toughest competition for McLaughlin came from Ruggiero in Mario Fiore's lightning fast #44. But the Fiore team was plagued with problems with engines, power steering, clutches, and tires. Some of this trouble may have been due to an overly ambitious schedule. Ruggiero and the #44 competed in 80 races of which only 31 were Tour races. He won two track championships and 23 races, but only three of his wins were in Modified Tour points races. After his stunning victory in the Ultra Race of Champions at Pocono in mid-September, Ruggiero regained the points lead by one point. Six days later, McLaughlin took back the lead with a victory at Shangri-La in Owego, New York, and he never again relinquished it in the three last races.

Although the points lead never left the hands of these two drivers, many other drivers distinguished themselves during the tour. Brian Ross finished third in points and won three races. Mike Stefanik won three. Any of these drivers could be next year's champion.

The 1988 NASCAR Winston Modified Tour champion, Mike McLaughlin, from Waterloo, New York. *Photo/Howard Hodge.*

Despite having only two weeks to prepare for the season, Mike McLaughlin completed the '88 tour with five victories, four Busch Poles, 15 top-five and 20 top-10 finishes in 24 races. Photo/Howard Hodge.

Billy Middleton had a scary moment during qualifying for the Winston Classic at Martinsville. After being hit by another car, the right rear wheel was ripped off, a flash fire erupted, and Billy made contact with the wall. Luckily, he wasn't hurt. Photo/Howard Hodge.

Mike McLaughlin and Reggie Ruggiero brought the championship battle into the pits. The toughest competition for McLaughlin came from Ruggiero in Mario Fiore's lightning-fast #44. But the Fiore team was plagued with problems with engines, power steering, clutches, and tires. Photo/Howard Hodge.

Richard Clark (#50) got all fours flying during Thompson's Winston 300. Although he landed on top of the wall, Clark managed to stay inside the track, escaping injury. Lloyd Agor (#78) was able to avoid an undue encounter with the acrobatic Clark. Photo/Howard Hodge.

Modifieds

Jamie Tomaino's crew is a blur of activity during the Pit Stop Competition at Riverside Park Speedway in Massachusetts. Photo/Howard Hodge.

Mike Ewanisko (#36) leads the pack at Martinsville. Ewanisko and Tom Baldwin (#7) won twice, while Mike Stefanik (#16) matched Ruggiero's three wins. McLaughlin, trailing the pack, won the race. Photo/Howard Hodge.

A blown engine resulted in a frightening flash fire on Roy Siedel's #77 Modified at Thompson. Siedel survived the conflagration without injury.
Photo/Howard Hodge.

Finishing third in points was Brian Ross (#69), led here by McLaughlin during the Winston 300. Brian Ross joined Ruggerio and Stefanik as three-time winners.
Photo/Howard Hodge.

Reggie Ruggiero (#44) is looking to pass Ed Flemke (#10), while Ted Christopher (#71) lays back. Ruggiero competed in 80 races of which only 31 were part of the Tour. He won two track championships and 23 events, but only three triumphs were Tour events.
Photo/Howard Hodge

ASA

by RON LEMASTERS, JR.
NATIONAL SPEED SPORT NEWS

BUTCH *MILLER SPENT MOST* of 1987 looking for ways to pass the time while making a shambles of the American Speed Association points battle. In 1988, however, Miller spent most of his time looking around for Harold Fair's menacing black Pontiac and was able to muster a late-season charge to hold off the determined Fair by 80 points and win his second straight ASA championship.

The hottest short track stock car driver in the country for the past two years, Miller rallied with four victories in the last six races to put the title out of reach for Fair, who had the best season of his career, finishing second.

Miller clinched the title after coming through a massive crash in the season finale, pushing his battered Chevrolet home third, ahead of 1987 ASA Rookie of the Year Ted Musgrave and Fair. It was the fourth time in seven years that the points championship has gone down to the last race of the season.

Winning six of the 16 races comprising the ASA's 20th Anniversary season, the 35-year-old Miller started from the Sunoco Pole Position 11 times in the SAI-Lane Automotive Chevrolet Camaro. His season earnings of $103,000 pushed his career total to over $500,000, only the fourth driver to join the "Half-Million Dollar Club." Other members are all-time ASA victory leader Bob Senneker, two-time ASA champ Dick Trickle and four-time champion Mike Eddy.

Series runner-up Fair won three races and two pole positions in his Hutter-Huisken Pontiac Grand Prix, breaking a 109-race winless streak in ASA competition dating back to 1982.

Butch Miller won six races and 10 pole positions to become the first driver in ASA Racing Series history to claim more than $100,000 in winnings in two consecutive seasons. He drove the #52 SAI-Lane Automotive Chevrolet owned by Leroy Throop and prepared by crew chief Kevin Hamlin to 15 wins of 31 races in two years. Photos/Don Thies (left), Phil Dullinger (bottom).

Jeff Neal was named 1988 Fel Pro Rookie of the Year. A third in the Pontiac Excitement 200 was his highest finish. Photo/Don Thies.

It's all in the family. Harold Alan Fair, crew chief for dad Harold, concentrates on the details. Photo/Don Thies.

Mike Garvey (#26) is ahead by a nose over Jody Ridley (#98), followed by Jeff Neal (#5) in the Nashville qualifier. ASA became the only major stock car sanctioning body to successfully match V6 and V8 engines in paved oval competition. Photo/Don Thies.

Toni Neal checks the progress of her husband, Jeff. Photo/Don Thies.

A spin by Mike Garvey (#26) precipitated a chain reaction in the Raider 300 at Salem Speedway. Victims of the pileup were Dennis Vogel (#51), Mark Beinlich (#59), Bruce Jeffords (#16) and Steve Seligman (#38). Photo/Don Thies.

Seven of ASA's 16 races were won with V6 engines. Dick Trickle scored four of those victories, to place fourth in points. Photo/Don Thies.

Musgrave improved upon a stellar rookie year by winning his first ASA race, the 18th annual Winchester 400 at Indiana's Winchester Speedway. Piloting his Baker Enterprises of Wisconsin Chevrolet, Musgrave was third in the final point standings with 1,965. Trickle, who had never ranked lower than second in the point standings since coming to ASA in 1980, finished fourth with 1,912 points, despite winning four races in the Coors Light Silver Bullet Chevrolet. Trickle hit his stride in August, tightening the already close points race even more by winning back-to-back events at Cayuga and Anderson (Indiana) Speedway. Eddy rebounded after a sub-par season in 1987 by finishing fifth with 1,733 points.

Eddy and Senneker, always near the top in ASA races, ended victory droughts in 1988. Eddy broke a 23-race winless streak with his victory in the Berlin 200, and Senneker topped the season-ending MidWest 300 at Salem Motor Speedway to bust his winless streak at 34 races. Senneker increased his all-time victory total to 59.

The ASA became the first major stock car sanctioning body to successfully match V6 and V8 engines in paved oval competition. Cars with V6 engines won seven (of 16) races and posted 28 top-five finishes.

Jeff Neal, son of Prototype Engines' head Ron Neal, took the Fel-Pro Rookie of the Year award by 204 points over Dan Christal.

Race City Speedway in Calgary, Alberta, was a new site for the ASA contingent in '88. The Canadian crowd was treated to action on the banking when Kevin Hampton (#40) spun and the rest of the pack, including Dave Jensen (#24), Gary St. Amant (#7), and Paul Dunbar (#46), tried to avoid him. Photo/Don Thies.

Two of ASA's finest, Butch Miller and Harold Fair, pace the field at Salem Speedway. For the seventh straight year, ASA distributed over $1 million in prize money and attendance increased by 7.4 percent. Photo/Don Thies.

In ASA's Gran Marque division, Ray Fullen ended a two-year streak of runner-up finishes by winning the points championship in the final race of the season. The Anderson, Indiana native won three races in his Weidner Chevrolet-Remline Tool Boxes Chevrolet Celebrity to edge hard-charging Rick Tomasik by 21 points.

Tomasik won three races, including the season-ending race at Salem. Tony Raines, Lonnie Rush, Jr. and Scott Keyser joined the lead pair as race winners. Raines was third in the point standings, followed by Keyser and Butch Lanum.

Ted Musgrave, last season's Rookie of the Year, romped to a single win at Winchester, grabbing third in the standings. Photo/Don Thies.

Musgrave's pit crew hustled to make a left-side tire change to maintain his lead in the Winchester 400. It worked. Photo/Don Thies.

Racing stock cars since 1963, Harold Fair's victory in the Raider 200 broke his 109-race winless streak. He went on to win two more races, challenging Butch Miller for the title right to the end. Miller was third in the season finale at Salem Speedway in a battered Chevy, while Fair finished fourth, assuring Miller the championship. Fair settled for second. Photo/Don Thies.

ARCA/Permatex Super Car Series

by RON DRAGER

TRACY *LESLIE HAD GONE* about as far as he could go in super late model competition in Canada, Ohio, Indiana, and his home state of Michigan. Winning on most paved short tracks he visited, he won consecutive championships at both tracks at which he competed on a weekly basis. Casting aside the virtual assurance of success inherent in following his established path, Leslie opted to venture into the ARCA Permatex Series.

After checking out the series, Leslie took advantage of an offer to drive a car fielded by Winston Cup veteran Dave Marcis in the 1986 and '87 ARCA season finales, held at Atlanta International Raceway. The experience almost sent the 30-year-old Mt. Clemens, Michigan driver home for good.

"In '86, we qualified in the top 10 at Atlanta but had motor problems and finished a bunch of laps down," said Leslie, owner of Leslie Tire Service in Mt. Clemens. "Then in '87, we qualified fifth and started strong. Seven laps into the race the transmission broke. I said to myself, 'That's it. I've spent a pile of money and can't even finish a race.' I was disillusioned."

But a call from Marcis to Leslie's shop in December of '87 made him reconsider. Leslie was offered a lucrative deal to campaign one of Marcis' cars in the ARCA superspeedway races if Leslie would undertake his own short track effort. Reaching an agreement with Marcis, Leslie opted to bolster his non-superspeedway program with a team of experienced, respected short-track veterans. The talents of Lee Leslie, Terry McKay and Robin Metdepenningen, holdovers from Leslie's successful late model operation were supplemented by Ed Howe, Don Biederman, Larry LaMay and car builder Chuck Carroll.

Leslie's extensive preparation was well rewarded. In his rookie season of 19 races, he rolled up a pair of pole qualifying runs, 11 top-10 finishes and four victories, plus leading an additional (to the four laps which earned him the checkered) 459 laps in seven other races. Utilizing Chevrolets and Pontiacs fielded by Marcis and his own Howe Racing Enterprises Oldsmobile, Leslie earned an ARCA record $93,200 in total team awards and the 1988 ARCA Permatex Series driving title.

Tracy Leslie's goal to become ARCA's Rookie of the Year was foiled when his outstanding 1988 season brought him the ARCA Permatex Super Car Series championship instead. He drove the South Limousine Sales Oldsmobile to four wins and two pole positions in nine starts. Photos/J.D. Scott (left), Jim Harris (bottom).

Championship runner-up Bob Keselowski led all drivers with five victories during the '88 season. At the wheel of the TRW Chevrolets owned and prepared by brother and ex-Winston Cup driver Ron Keselowski, Bob won more pole positions and led more laps in 1988 than any other series driver.

Third man in the standings, Grant Adcox of Chattanooga, Tennessee had his best career Permatex Series points finish. His two '88 wins brought his all-time leading career ARCA superspeedway victory total to eight. Driving the Herb Adcox Chevrolets fielded by his father, Adcox has now led more laps (731) in more races (20) on superspeedways than any driver in ARCA history.

Defending Permatex Series champion Bill Venturini continued to show the consistency which has landed him in the top five in final series points for the fifth consecutive season. Venturini piloted the Amoco Ultimate-Rain X Chevrolets owned by his wife Cathy and crewed by the all-female Ultra Blue pit crew to seven top-five and 12 top-10 finishes in 19 starts.

Veteran Jerry Churchill, who ran his first ARCA race in 1970, had his most successful season with a fifth place points finish, outside-pole qualifying runs at Atlanta and Talladega, and top-five finishes at Daytona and Talladega.

In year-end special awards, Chevrolet won the ARCA Manufacturer's Championship for the second straight season; Bobby Gerhart of Lebanon, Pennsylvania won the Dayton Enterprises ARCA Rookie of the Year honors; Veteran car owner and engine builder Charlie Newby won the ARCA Mechanic of the Year award; Grant Adcox received the Sportsmanship award; and Mike Fry was named the Reed Cams Most Improved Driver.

Grant Adcox (#2) and Charlie Glotzbach (#49) bring the field down for the start of the 25th annual Daytona ARCA 200. Mickey Gibbs took the win. The '88 ARCA series saw 136 different drivers from 24 states, two Canadian provinces and Australia compete for a record $1,173,600. Photo/Courtesy of Int'l Speedway Corp.

The ageless Red Farmer (l.) of Hueytown, Alabama, gives advice to Patty Moise on running Talladega, as Farmer's car owner Davey Allison looks on. It obviously worked.
Photo/Jim Harris.

Red Farmer (#28) leads Patty Moise (#37) at Talladega. Patty Moise turned heads by planting her Buick on the pole for both Permatex Series races at Alabama International Motor Speedway.
Photo/Courtesy of Int'l Speedway Corp.

Mickey Gibbs bookended the season by winning the series opener at Daytona and the Atlanta Journal 500k finale. Photo/Jim Harris.

Defending champ Bill Venturini continued to show the consistency which has landed him in the top five in final series points for the fifth straight season. Boasting an all-female pit crew, he was fifth for the year. Photo/Courtesy of Int'l Speedway Corp.

Extending his superspeedway mastery with wins at Atlanta and Talladega, Grant Adcox (#2) increased his all-time leading career ARCA superspeedway total to eight. The Chattanooga driver ended up second in points. Photo/Courtesy of Int'l Speedway Corp.

All Pro

Comfortable in the cockpit prior to a 200-lap April event at Hialeah Speedway, Jody Ridley went on to win five races and the 1988 All Pro Super Series championship, his second. Photo/Brian McLeod.

Despite a relative lack of finances, experience and equipment, Clay Brown became the 1988 All Pro Super Series Brodix Heads Rookie of the Year. Photo/Brian McLeod.

Ridley began his quest for a second consecutive title from a unique vantage point after an early spin in the opening race at Five Flags Speedway. Photo/Brian McLeod.

NASCAR/Charlotte-Daytona Dash

by ANDY HALL

*F*OR *THE SECOND STRAIGHT* year, Larry Caudill of North Wilkesboro, North Carolina, reigned as the 1988 champion of NASCAR's Charlotte/Daytona Dash Series for sub-compact, four-cylinder race cars.

But it was the emergence of two young stars that attracted a great deal of attention to the Dash Series in 1988. Both were unique and both earned their headlines.

While Caudill was winning nine of the 15 races in the series and wrapping up the points championship by a comfortable margin, many eyes were watching 23-year-old Shawna Robinson of Des Moines, Iowa, and 17-year-old Todd Cray of Trenton, New Jersey. Robinson and Cray battled all season for the series' Rookie of the Year award, but that battle was secondary to the shot in the arm the series received in terms of attention generated by the two.

Robinson, a former diesel truck racer, drove in her first stock car race in February of 1988 at Daytona International Speedway and finished third. Then, in only her sixth race, she drove to victory on a Friday night at the 1/3-mile New Asheville (North Carolina) Speedway on June 10, making her the first woman to win a feature race in NASCAR's 40-year history. The win made the national wire services and her story was featured coast-to-coast.

In the 15 events comprising the Dash Series, Robinson finished in second place once and third place three times, scoring a total of seven top-five finishes. She wound up third in the point standings behind Caudill and long-time veteran Mickey York of Asheboro, North Carolina. She also won the rookie crown, making her only the second female titlist in NASCAR history. The other was fellow Dash competitor Karen Schulz, who won the award in 1986.

Cray, who won hundreds of races in go karts and quarter midgets until he got too old for those forms of racing, drove in four events in 1987, then tackled the Dash Series full time in 1988. He won quickly at Hickory, North Carolina, in the third race of the season, then won again later at Myrtle Beach, South Carolina. Although he did not score as many consistently high finishes as Robinson, he did finish fourth in the point standings, only 16 tallies behind Robinson.

For repeat champion Caudill, the season was also remarkable in that he did not even have a full-time ride when the season started. He had won the 1987 title as a teammate to Schulz, but the Schulz team decided to field only one car in 1988, leaving Caudill looking. He put together a deal with long-time sponsor Douglas & Son Trucking for a few races but, after winning the season opener at Daytona, the team came together.

For the second straight year, Larry Caudill reigned as the 1988 champion of NASCAR's Charlotte/Daytona Dash Series. Photo/Courtesy of Int'l Speedway Corp.

Caudill went on to win two other superspeedway races at Charlotte Motor Speedway, giving him a sweep of the series' events on tracks of a mile or more in length. He also won on several short tracks, including Orange County Speedway (Rougemont, North Carolina), Summerville (South Carolina) Speedway, Langley Speedway (Hampton, Virginia), Anderson (South Carolina) Speedway, Hickory Speedway, and Lanier Raceway (Gainesville, Georgia).

Runner-up York did not take a race win, but had nine top-five finishes, including three second places. Series rookie Stephen Durham of Williamsburg, Virginia, scored a win at Nashville, Tennessee, while 1987 Rookie of the Year Andy Belmont of Feasterville, Pennsylvania, won at Myrtle Beach and Richmond, Virginia.

Shawna Robinson (#21) emerged as not only the Rookie of the Year, the second time in NASCAR history that a woman has done so, but as the first woman in NASCAR's 40-year history to win a feature race! A former diesel truck racer, Robinson also ended up third in points. Photo/Howard Hodge.

At the Daytona opener, Larry Caudill (#77) leads the pack onto the front straight. Caudill won nine of the 15 races in this series for sub-compact, four-cylinder race cars. Photo/Courtesy of Int'l Speedway Corp.

NASCAR/Winston Racing Series

by ANDY HALL

A *23-YEAR-OLD RISING STAR* from the Charleston-area town of Moncks Corner, South Carolina, became the leader of all NASCAR weekly short track racers by winning the NASCAR Winston Racing Series national championship in 1988.

Robert Powell won the Southeast Region championship, the same title he won in 1986. This time, though, his record was the best among the other regional champions. Powell won a sizzling .741 percent of his races en route to winning the national title, his first. He won 23 of the 31 races in which he competed during 1988 on asphalt short tracks in Anderson, Myrtle Beach and Summerville, South Carolina. The championship was worth $47,000 in post-season awards.

In 1988, the Winston Racing Series divided the country into six regions, with drivers at NASCAR-sanctioned tracks competing for regional championships under a uniform system that awarded points based on their best 20 finishes during a 22-week season that began in April. At season's end, the winning percentages of the six regional champions were compared to determine the national champion.

Asphalt racer Glenn Gault of Hubbard, Ohio, won the Northeast Region title, racing at Jennerstown and Clearfield Speedways in Pennsylvania. His winning percentage of .594 was second to Powell, nationally.

Other regional champions were Central Region titlist Dale Fischlein of Davenport, Iowa; James Cline of Anniston, Alabama, in the Sunbelt Region; Mid-Atlantic Region champion Robert Pressley of Asheville, North Carolina; and Ed Sans, Jr., of Santa Clara, California, top competitor in the Pacific Coast Region. Pressley was the lone repeat 1987 champion.

Powell became the seventh different national champion in the seven-year-old Winston Racing Series. In 1989, the series will include some 85 weekly race tracks across the country, divided into eight regions.

By winning the NASCAR Winston Racing Series national championship in 1988, Robert Powell became the seventh different champion in the seven-year-old series. Photo/David Allio-Courtesy of R.J. Reynolds.

Powell became the leader of all NASCAR weekly short-track racers in his Camaro by taking first in a sizzling .741 percent of his races. He won 23 of the 31 races in which he competed on asphalt short tracks in the Southeast. Photo/David Allio-Courtesy of R.J. Reynolds.

Glenn Gault captured the 1988 Northeast Region championship and second in national points. Photo/David Allio-Courtesy of R.J. Reynolds.

The Central Region championship went to Dale Fischlein, who placed third nationally. Photo/David Allio-Courtesy of R.J. Reynolds.

Robert Pressley of Asheville, North Carolina, won his second straight Mid-Atlantic Region crown. Photo/David Allio-Courtesy of R.J. Reynolds.

Taking the title by only five points, Ed Sans, Jr. was named the 1988 Pacific Coast Region champion. Photo/David Allio-Courtesy of R.J. Reynolds.

Anniston, Alabama's James Cline, Jr. earned the 1988 Sunbelt Region championship. Photo/David Allio-Courtesy of R.J. Reynolds.

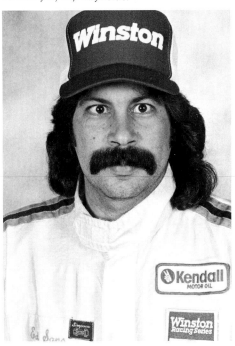

Commentary:

SAFETY FIRST

by MIKE HARRIS
MOTORSPORTS EDITOR, THE ASSOCIATED PRESS

THE BEST MOMENTS IN auto racing are doorhandle-to-doorhandle action and dramatic, gut-wrenching finishes.

The worst moments come when cars veer out of control and the lives of drivers, crew members, track workers, officials or spectators are endangered.

Some of the most heart-stopping moments of my life—professional and personal—have been those instants, frozen in time, when a major crash has put a person or persons in real and imminent danger.

Forever etched in my memory are those few moments in October of 1981 at Phoenix, when the yellow Chaparral Indy car of Johnny Rutherford became airborne, upside down, with the three-time Indianapolis 500 champion a helpless passenger.

There is also that instant of very real fear at Talladega, Alabama, in May of 1987 when it appeared that Bobby Allison's 3,500-pound stock car was about to fly into the packed main grandstand while traveling at something approaching 200 MPH.

I remember vividly a 500-mile Indy car event at Brooklyn, Michigan, in which Irishman Derek Daly crashed hard, virtually head-on in Turn Three, crushing his feet and sitting helplessly in the car while safety people pried him out.

In each of those situations—just three of many that come quickly to mind from 20 years of covering the sport—the fates, Lady Luck, chance or circumstance, whatever you believe in, kept the incident from becoming a tragedy.

Rutherford credited his helmet and the integrity of the car with keeping him alive, well and ready to race another day.

Allison's car tore down nearly 100 yards of steel reinforced safety fence but stayed out of the stands. The aging and barely adequate fencing was quickly replaced by Talladega officials, while NASCAR officials took immediate steps to slow down the cars at the Alabama track and at Daytona International Speedway, the two stock car facilities where speeds over 200 MPH had become commonplace.

Daly is able to walk, and still able to compete, because a specialist was on hand to somehow keep the circulation going in his battered feet while he still slumped in the wreckage.

But, safety is a constant and sometimes overlooked battle.

Incidents like those described above, or the crash at Pocono International Raceway this past June in which Allison suffered critical injuries, are what raise questions—at least briefly. But the problems are always there, attested to by the constantly rising insurance rates for race tracks and the ever-present insurance company representatives, who tell the tracks what they can and cannot do, where people can and cannot go.

Ironically, despite faster and faster cars, auto racing has never been safer.

No less an authority than A.J. Foyt, Jr., the man who has conquered Indy, Daytona, Le Mans, Sebring, and just about every other race track of note, says, "The cars I drive now are much safer than the ones I was racing in 20 years ago because they are better balanced, easier to drive and give you a better chance of walking away if something does happen."

Fire, which was the greatest enemy of the race driver when Foyt first put on a helmet and stepped into the cockpit of a race car, has been virtually eliminated in the past 15 years by Goodyear's crash-worthy fuel cell, a device invented to keep American helicopters from catching fire while being shot at in Vietnam.

The drivers still realize, though, that anything can happen when you hurl your body around at high speed. But, Rutherford represents a lot of the participants when he says, "Nobody ever put a gun to my head to make me get in a race car. I do it because I want to do it."

The biggest safety question raised in recent years is what are the tracks and sanctioning bodies doing to stay on top of the situation?

Most of the top tracks in America have done the right thing—replacing dangerous fencing on ovals with concrete walls, extending runoff areas, eliminating hazzards on the fastest parts of road circuits, and generally listening and acting upon complaints from the drivers.

However, not everybody has done all that can be done to insure the safety of participants.

While CART and the NHRA have the Horton Safety Team and the Safety Safari, respectively, NASCAR still leaves it up to each of its sanctioned tracks to make its own safety arrangements.

CART and the NHRA both have top-grade safety equipment, trained personnel and doctors schooled in handling trauma injuries on hand at every event. Some NASCAR tracks have equipment and personnel which match those of the NHRA and CART. But there are several NASCAR facilities which could prove woefully inadequate.

Bill France, Jr., president of NASCAR, has said that the difference in the licensing of doctors from state to state; the requirements of insurance; and the way NASCAR is set up, keep the stock car sanctioning body from setting up a safety team of its own.

Even the close call for Allison, one of NASCAR's best known and best loved stars, did not shake the Daytona Beach-based group into action.

Pocono is one of the few tracks at which NASCAR runs that has a fully-trained emergency medical team and keeps a lifeline helicopter on hand for emergency transport to a nearby hospital. People close to Allison credit those two factors with keeping the Hueytown, Alabama, driver alive last June.

It's only been in the last couple of years that one major NASCAR facility has stopped using rented vans with magnetic red-cross signs on the sides and medically untrained drivers during its races, replacing them with a handful of real ambulances and trained crews.

But in one recent event—witnessed by yours truly— a wrecker reached a crashed car, the driver still slumped unconscious inside, before a safety vehicle arrived. The driver of the wrecker began hooking up the battered car, ignoring the injured driver who, it turned out, had a concussion.

At another track this past season, during a practice session, one of NASCAR's stars sat trapped in his demolished car while a fellow driver, with no medical training or practiced safety skills, directed a group of crewmen and track officials in their efforts to remove him.

Time is of the essence in these incidents. Speed and training save lives in emergency situations.

In other major forms of racing, including Formula One, safety equipment and trained personnel often arrive at the site of an accident almost before the damaged car or cars stop moving. Once they get there, they know exactly what to do.

That isn't simply a good idea whose time has come. It is an outright necessity.

The sport as a whole has continued to improve its safety record year after year. There is still room for improvement. Here is hoping that everybody gets the message, and soon.

Nobody wants to be left with only the option of saying, "I told you so!"

Michael S. Harris

NASCAR/Winston West

by OWEN KEARNS, JR.

IT'S TRUE, DYNASTIES ARE built a season at a time. But the record books of the future may well show that 1988 marked the beginning of the dynasty of Roy Smith, Jackie Johnson and Rabanco Racing owner Warren Razore.

It wasn't so much that the trio mowed down their competition in NASCAR's Winston West series. Young Chad Little did the same thing in 1987 and, the season before, racing grandfather Hershel McGriff ended the campaign in similar fashion. Neither Little nor McGriff repeated as champions but there's ample evidence upon which to argue that Canadian Smith, who won consecutive Winston West championships from 1980 through 1982, is in a much stronger position.

But first, consider that the driver, his crew chief Johnson and car owner Razore pretty much reached consensus during the off-season that, because the team hadn't jelled in 1987, each would be better off with someone else. Razore, who'd found victory circle just once in three seasons, had about concluded that there were other, more pleasurable pursuits than automobile racing. But the 1988 season, after the trio had agreed to extend a shaky relationship, proved to be a perfect case of the Phoenix rising from the ashes.

Smith, now in his forties, raced with the gusto of the Sprint car driver he'd been a decade before. Johnson's Western Peterbilt Ford Thunderbirds, powered by T.O.E.-built engines, were the cars to beat from the first race to the last. And Razore, a Seattle businessman, learned to smile broadly after Smith produced the year's first victory—and then the second—and, finally, a championship-clinching third.

A soft-spoken commercial fisherman, Smith calls it a matter of improved communication. Bringing together a championship driver, a winning crew chief and an owner with the resources to excel doesn't, Smith suggests, guarantee an unbeatable combination. They have to get to know one another. A great marriage may result but, on the other hand, the relationship just as easily can wind up in divorce court.

"Jackie (Johnson) was used to setting up the car for Derrike Cope (the 1984 Winston West series Rookie of the Year, now graduated to Winston Cup) and I liked a different kind of feel," recalls Smith. "We finally were able to sit down and talk things out. Everybody gave a little bit and, well, you can see the results."

Roy Smith (l.), the 1988 Winston West Series champion. Jackie Johnson's Western Peterbilt Ford Thunderbird (below), powered by a T.O.E.-built engine, was the car to beat from the first race to the last. Photos/Cole Porter (left), Taylors Photography (bottom).

Defending titlist Chad Little is beat out of the pits by Bill Schmitt at Evergreen Speedway. Schmitt was second to Little in the Motorcraft 500 and second in the season standings. Photo/Cole Porter.

Smith was a threat to win all six of Winston West's stand-alone dates but settled for a .500 batting average. He claimed the rich Spokane Grand Prix street race, winning the Budweiser 300 for the second time. And he won twice at Bakersfield, California's half-mile Mesa Marin Raceway, lapping the field in May and beating Winston Cup visitor Rusty Wallace in August. With that victory, he concurrently celebrated his 44th birthday and captured the series crown.

Tire problems robbed him of three more victories, although each wound up as a third place finish. His rubber worn, Smith spun from the lead of the season opener at Sonoma, California with fewer than four laps to go. Handling kept him from the winner's circle at Portland, Oregon and flats dropped him from contention in the Motorcraft 500 at Monroe, Washington.

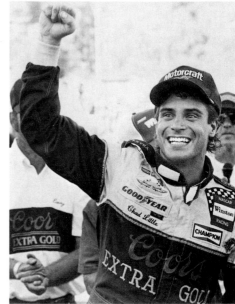

Winning only once in '88 following a celebrated 1987, Little will move into Winston Cup for '89. Photo/Cole Porter.

Little's crew gave him rapid service on his way to his second Motorcraft 500 win, but Little was unable to come close to his '87 performance, placing third in points. Photo/Cole Porter.

Observed Smith, "I feel better for Warren and the group than for me because their time, effort and money finally has paid off. One thing that makes me feel the best is that, at my age, you always wonder, 'Do you still have it?' I guess this proves I do."

Schmitt, a 52 year-old lumberman from Redding, California, beat Smith at Sears Point International Raceway and was the series runner-up. Little, who will move to Winston Cup in '89, saved his up-and-down season with a second Motorcraft 500 victory and was third in the final standings. Fourth and fifth ranked were 58 year-old J.C. Danielsen (competing in his third decade of Winston West) and the 60 year-old McGriff who was shut out of victory circle for the first time since 1984. Bob Howard, a general contractor from Colorado, took Rookie of the Year honors, leading both Bakersfield races and finishing fifth in the second Bakersfield round.

The oldest driver on the Winston West circuit, McGriff, was shut out of victory circle in '88 for the first time since 1984. Photo/Taylors Photography.

Hershel McGriff is hugged by his daughter. The combined years of McGriff, who was fifth for the year, and fourth-placer Jim Danielson exceed the century mark by a decade! Photo/Cole Porter.

Chad Little and Bill Schmitt made a sandwich out of Jack Sellers (#41). Photo/Cole Porter.

Bill Schmitt won the Sears Point opener, sat on the pole for the Motorcraft 500 and came within a broken axle and a few laps of winning it. Photo/Taylors Photography.

Spokane hosted the Series' first street-course race. Scott Gaylord took to the safety of the tire wall after plowing into it. Photo/Cole Porter.

Winston West champion Roy Smith leads the pack down Spokane's Boy Scout Boulevard. Photo/Cole Porter.

Mark Walbridge slammed into the inside wall on the front stretch at the Motorcraft 500. His car nearly broken in half by the impact, Walbridge escaped uninjured. Photo/Cole Porter.

NASCAR/Winston Cup

by **RANDY HALLMAN**
THE RICHMOND NEWS LEADER

WE START WITH YOU, Bobby Allison.

The supreme irony of the 1988 major league stock car racing season is that you have forgotten most of it. Your story is the salient memory of the year, what we will remember when the rest has faded into trivia. The pain you suffered—and the subsequent outpouring of emotion from competitors and fans—gave a sense of perspective to an otherwise bizarre year.

Long before this season you were accorded larger-than-life status in the sport—the quintessential battler, digging in against other drivers, against the NASCAR autocracy, against age itself. And now you struggle to recover from a crash that broke your bones and looted your memory.

Maybe this account of the season will make it easier to call up recollections of your own. Fair warning: On first hearing you will not believe some of what went on.

This much you can believe—when you put your weight on that cane, when you feel the residue of pain deep in your knitting bones, when your speech comes a half-tick slow—you took a bad hit, Bobby.

Pocono International Raceway.

June 19.

First lap.

Tunnel Turn.

One of your tires was going flat. You twisted sideways in front of traffic. Jocko Maggiacomo's car slammed into your Buick—a driver's side T-bone. You were unconscious, and thoroughly broken up. "Critical condition with a head injury and other injuries," the hospital said. We feared...well, you know what we feared.

More than two months passed before you were able to hold a press conference and tell us how much of your memory had been jarred loose.

We were taken aback. We had expected you to have no recollection of the wreck. That happens to drivers all the time. But you couldn't remember winning the Daytona 500 in February. You said you couldn't call up the last eight or nine years. The '80s were missing from your files.

Even 1983, the season you won your lone championship—gone, as if it had never happened, you said.

Yet, somewhere in there the memories lie waiting. You told us you were beginning to remember things—odd bits, like where you steered your boat in a fishing tournament, or who your companions were at a dinner party.

Where to begin recounting the 1988 Winston Cup season? First there was the celebrated urine sample, and then Goodyear went flat in the tire war, and then...

By snatching the 1988 NASCAR Winston Cup national championship away from Rusty Wallace, Bill Elliott collected a season total of $1,554,639—a record fourth consecutive year he has surpassed $1 million in winnings. Photo/Jim Harris.

Elliott's 24-point margin over Wallace made the title chase the third closest in NASCAR history. Elliott parked his Coors Ford in six victory lanes to earn his first-ever Winston Cup crown. Photo/Ken Brown-Competition Photographers.

But wait, no point in taxing your credulity so soon. Let's go with the straight stuff first.

Bill Elliott won the Winston Cup championship this season, holding off Rusty Wallace after Dale Earnhardt's bid for a third straight title faded in the stretch.

The names must perplex you if that eight-year memory gap is complete. They're part of a whole new cast of stars in the sport. When the '80s began Bill Elliott was still a part-timer from north Georgia who had exactly one top-five finish to his name. Earnhardt had shown promise as 1979 Rookie of the Year. Wallace was just another Midwest talent who hadn't hit the big-time yet. Elliott started winning in 1983. Earnhardt's star rose in the mid-'80s. Wallace won a few races in '86 and '87, then blossomed in '88.

In 1985, Elliott had one of the great seasons in motorsports history—11 victories, 11 poles, most laps led, etc., etc.,—but failed to win the championship. Elliott learned the same lesson you had learned in 1972, Bobby, when you had 10 wins and 12 second-place finishes in 31 starts—but lost the title to Richard Petty with 8 wins and nine seconds.

NASCAR's point system does not always reward the spectacular season. It does always reward perseverance. The driver who goes full-tilt to hoist himself from fifth to first gains 25 points. The driver who has trouble early but patches his car and limps through a race—never passing a car, but taking advantage of attrition to move from 35th to 15th—gains 60 points.

Winning is not as important as avoiding a bad finish.

Miller Beer spraying in celebration, Bobby Allison enjoys the perks of a well-earned victory. Bobby narrowly defeated his son Davey to capture his third Daytona 500 in February, then fought for his life later in the season following a devastating wreck at Pocono.
Photo/Bill Stahl.

Although only a bridesmaid, Rusty Wallace enjoyed six wins and his best Winston Cup career finish. Photo/Tom Riles.

The season-long skirmish between Elliott and Wallace finally culminated at the finale. Rusty won the Atlanta Journal 500, but Bill's 11th-place finish was strong enough to land him the championship. Here, at Phoenix, they went nose to nose seeking those precious points. Photo/Phil Dullinger.

So in 1988, when Elliott found himself sitting on a comfortable 127-point lead with six races to go, he did the prudent thing. He quit taking chances and started nursing that lead.

Wallace did what he could to make things interesting. He came on like gangbusters to win four of the last five events, three times making up deficits of a lap or more. That gave him six victories for the year. Elliott, who had done his charging earlier and won six times himself, protected his lead with a string of modest finishes, not better than fourth.

Come November and the final race in Atlanta, Elliott needed only to finish 18th or better to clinch the title. Wallace came to town breathing fire. He declared that he was out to lead the most laps and win the race, practically daring Elliott to chase him and give the fans the finish they deserved.

Wallace tried to appeal to Elliott's pride, his competitive spirit, his manhood—to push whatever button it took to get Drawlin' Bill from Dawsonville riled. Wallace wanted Elliott to feel the need to show his prowess at his home track, to battle for superiority— and perhaps to pay for it by blowing an engine or otherwise taking himself out.

Elliott politely declined. He never led a lap, never really got close. While Wallace made good his promise to dominate and win the race, Elliott set a soporific pace and finished 11th. About the only time his Thunderbird and Wallace's Pontiac were close to each other was when Wallace lapped him.

There was a hue and cry from some expert commentators that Elliott had cheapened the championship by winning in an unaggressive fashion, that he should have capped the season with an all-out effort.

(Memo to the aforementioned expert commentators: Don't talk to Elliott, talk to NASCAR, which devised the confounded point system. Elliott had been aggressive in 1985. That was fun, but this time out he wanted to be champion, and by season's end, fun wasn't on the agenda.)

"I was pretty much just setting a pace," said the newly crowned champion, trying not to sound apologetic. "It certainly does make for quite a long day, that's for certain. All year long didn't take as long as this particular race did. Consistency is a hard row to hoe."

Famed crew chief Harry Hyde (l.) gave Ken Schrader some advice before the spring Talladega event. The words sunk in later, however, as Kenny won the summer race at the Alabama speedway. Hyde will take over Bobby Hillin, Jr.'s team in '89. Photo/Jim Harris.

Dale Earnhardt just barely avoided serious damage to his Goodwrench Chevy when he came in contact with a wayward wheel upon exiting the Atlanta pits behind Rusty Wallace. Photo/Jim Harris.

Davey Allison crawls from his crippled Ford after he crashed in Turn Two of the Atlanta 500. He was uninjured. Photo/Jim Harris.

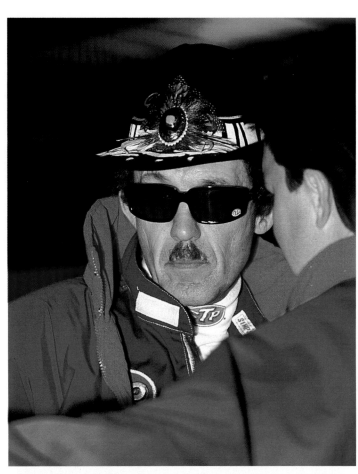

"King" Richard Petty, seven-time winner of the Daytona 500, hasn't won a race since July, 1984. An awful lot of people watched him struggle to regain his winning touch and wondered if he ought to pack it in. Photo/Tom Riles.

This blown tire at Charlotte was one of Richard Petty's least disastrous events of the year. Early in the Daytona 500, he took a wild ride along the spectator fence, his Pontiac doing a harrowing toe dance on its front corner before disintegrating and showering car parts on the scattering fans. He escaped unhurt, but made a mandatory visit to the local hospital vowing to return to the race. Photo/Crisp Images.

It was also an uphill climb for three-time defending Winston Cup champion Dale Earnhardt. He won only three times, at Atlanta, Martinsville and Bristol, and settled for third in the standings. Photo/Dick Conway.

Davey Allison's crewman signals the Havoline Ford into the pits at Daytona. Photo/Crisp Images.

Consistency and prudence were the watchwords for the end of the season, but the year began under headlines about a driver with a reputation for being spectacularly inconsistent and imprudent. It was inevitable that Tim Richmond and NASCAR would have a showdown.

The tour's most exciting figure with seven victories in 1986, Richmond missed most of the 1987 season because of a lingering illness. He maintained his problem was pneumonia, a claim never documented. Rumors persisted that the illness was drug-related and/or that he had AIDS.

NASCAR decreed that, starting in 1988, drivers could be required to take drug tests. When Richmond came to Daytona in February, NASCAR handed him not a registration form, but a vial to fill for a urinalysis.

NASCAR soon announced Richmond had tested positive for banned drugs and could not race again until he produced a clean sample.

And what, exactly, were the offending substances? It took NASCAR nearly a week to get more specific test results and announce that Richmond's urine showed unacceptably high levels of two over-the-counter drugs—pseudoephedrine and ibuprofen. He was getting busted for Sudafed abuse and Advil overdose.

Richmond insisted the test results were erroneous, though he admitted he had been using medication to fight a cold. He submitted another urine sample. This one tested clean.

NASCAR wasn't satisfied. Officials now demanded to see the medical records documenting Richmond's persistent illness. Richmond hired a lawyer—none other than Barry Ivan Slotnick, the defender of Subway Vigilante Bernhard Goetz.

Gritting his teeth no doubt, Rusty Wallace (l.) accepts a handshake from the newly-crowned Winston Cup champion, Bill Elliott. Photo/Al Steinberg.

Wheeling the Budweiser Chevrolet, Terry Labonte saw the inside of victory circle only once, at North Wilkesboro in April, ending up fourth for the year. Photo/Randy McKee.

Pit signs not only direct the drivers into their proper pits, but help promote the sponsors, too. Photos/Taylors Photography (bottom), Ken Brown-Competition Photographers (below).

The tire companies stole the show in '88. Hoosier, who doesn't make street-car tires, came on the scene with a vengeance. Goodyear said they were backing out, then they stayed. At Pocono the Goodyears were too fat, and at Watkins Glen NASCAR claimed the Hoosiers gained a little too much width. It was a "pick 'em as you see 'em" kind of season. At some race tracks the Hoosiers worked best, at others it was the Goodyears. The teams made their choices as they saw fit. But, in the end, Goodyear came out on top. Score 20 wins for the Akron brand, nine for the purple people. Photos/Taylors Photography (top), Jim Harris (above).

In the race for the coveted manufacturers championship, Ford—despite Bill Elliott's six wins—lost the title to Chevrolet by two points! Photo/Bill Stahl.

The Winston Cup series reached a milestone by drawing over 3 million spectators in '88, once again the world leader in total attendance. Stock car racing continues to be a prime arena for promoting commercial products. Photo/Bill Stahl.

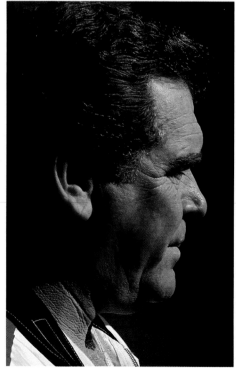

Soft-spoken Buddy Baker will retire as a driver but will return as a car owner in 1989. Photo/Rich Chenet.

The '88 season was the last for Hardee's Olds driver Cale Yarborough. He'll play the role of car owner in future seasons. Photo/David Taylor.

Slotnick contended Richmond had a right to keep his medical records private. NASCAR and Slotnick stared each other down. Neither relented, and the Daytona 500 went on without Richmond. During the early laps, a light plane flew over the grandstands, trailing a banner with the plaintive words, "Fans, I miss you. Tim Richmond."

For months there were rumors that the impasse would be solved and Richmond would be back. But Richmond didn't race in 1988. Eventually, he filed a $20 million lawsuit against NASCAR.

The incident begs a number of questions. Did NASCAR test anybody else during the year? Did anybody else test positive? Is the drug policy still in effect?

If there were other tests, those tests were kept quiet. NASCAR declines to comment.

As for Richmond, he has virtually disappeared from the public eye, making him, once again, the tour's chief source of rumor.

Is he in ill health again? Did he join the motorcycle crowd's bacchanalian revels last March in Daytona Beach? Has he repaired to the condo in south Florida where he convalesced before? Was he seen in Charlotte, gaunt and pale?

The mystery deepens.

Compared to the Byzantine Richmond affair, the tire war was simple. Two tire makers battled for supremacy, and good old all-American free-market competition brought out the worst in both.

It was not a renewal of the Firestone-Goodyear war of the '60s, Bobby. This time Hoosier Racing Tire, a relatively tiny company that doesn't even produce a passenger tire, took on Goodyear Tire & Rubber Company.

Goodyear, unaccustomed to serious competition for nearly 20 years, had been producing tires with the emphasis on safety rather than speed. But Goodyear was shaken out of its complacency when Hoosier-shod cars won three of the first five 1988 races—despite the fact that virtually all the major teams had remained loyal to Goodyear.

Goodyear engineers went to work on new compounds to meet the challenge. Hoosier, trying to maintain its early advantage, continued to design more speed into its tires.

Ernie Elliott built the engines that powered the championship-winning #9 Coors Ford. Photo/Jim Harris.

Budding stock car racers go for the gold (or perhaps the cookies) at the Watkins Glen "kiddie" race. Photo/Tom Bernhardt.

Bill Elliott's army marches on the victory lane where he was presented the Winston Cup trophy. Isn't that Rod Campbell, head of Ford's motorsports publicity effort, holding a placard? Guess who instigated this little promo! Photo/Jim Harris.

Benny Parsons might be thinking he should retire more often as he bids farewell to the Unocal Racestoppers at his final race. Photo/Jim Harris.

At The Glen, Benny confronted the guardrail, as Bobby Hillin, Jr. passed by. Photo/Stan Clinton.

Fuel cans at the ready, pit crews service their cars amidst "chaos" as drivers scream into the pits during a caution period. Winston Cup crews are, without question, the world's finest. Photos/Doc Waldrop, Werner Fritz (inset).

In the push to go faster, both companies sacrificed durability and shaved the margin of safety ever thinner. Blistered and blown tires were commonplace. In May, Goodyear admitted the tire it had developed for the Charlotte 600-miler was unsafe and withdrew, leaving the field to Hoosier. However, Hoosier's apparent coup turned sour during the race, when blowouts precipitated a rash of wrecks.

The two companies continued to search for any advantage—to the point of embarrassment. In June, Goodyear was excluded from a race because its tires were wider than NASCAR rules allowed. In August, Hoosier was banned from a race for the same infraction.

By season's end, Goodyear had regained the upper hand, and for the year, Goodyear scored 20 wins to Hoosier's nine. One wonders how the totals would have read if, instead of Goodyear's all-stars battling Hoosier's pick-up squad, the talent had been evenly divided.

Some of the best and worst of '88...

Best comeback to competition: Neil Bonnett's two early-season victories at Richmond and Rockingham.

That's right, Bobby, your good friend and neighbor from Hueytown, Alabama, had to make a comeback, and he said you were a crucial factor in that comeback. He had shattered his right femur in a racing crash late in 1987. He was ready to quit, he said, until you talked to him last winter.

He limps, and his bone is held together with enough screws to open a hardware store—but he can still drive. Although his season leveled off after the two wins, he gave a good enough account of himself to land a ride with the brothers Wood, Glen and Leonard, for 1989.

If you're not served in five minutes, the pizza is free. Make it about 18 seconds for a tire change and refueling. Morgan Shepherd's crew are pros. Photo/R.L. Montgomery.

Harry Gant gets a wheel up on the
competition in the Skoal Bandit Chevy.
Gant scored only three top-10 finishes.
Photo/Stan Clinton.

Talk about billboards in motion! Every
inch of a Winston Cup car, save the
number area, is available to commercial
sponsors, from beer—to motor oil—to
soap suds. Photo/Sidell Tilghman.

Blood, sweat and cheers.

Winning six consecutive NASCAR Winston Cup Manufacturer's Championships
requires more than fast cars, so Chevrolet wants to thank the teams that endured 1988's
scorching heat and competitive pressure. Congratulations to Hendrick Motorsports,
Junior Johnson Associates, Mach 1 Racing, Marcis Auto Racing, RCR Racing Enterprises
and the entire Bowtie Brigade for helping us reach
this unprecedented landmark.

THE *Heartbeat* OF AMERICA IS WINNING

Chevrolet's six consecutive Winston Manufacturer's Championship Cups.

Dana Patten got sideways in Turn Four at Michigan. He slid into the infield but caused no caution flag to appear, and continued the race. Photo/Bob Brodbeck.

Two Chevys from Rick Hendrick's stable go at it at Dover. Ken Schrader (#25) won at Talladega in July, Darrell Waltrip (#17) took Charlotte and Martinsville. Schrader out-scored Waltrip in season points by coming up fifth to Darrell's seventh. Photo/Ken Brown-Competition Photographers.

The season lost some of its luster when Bobby Allison wrecked hard at Pocono. While the world prayed and waited for word, Bobby lay in critical condition. More than two months passed before he was able to hold a press conference and assure his fans and friends that he'd be okay. Son Davey came to a stop at the crash site to check on his dad. Photo/Tom Bernhardt.

Running out of gas on the cool-off lap at Michigan, Ricky Rudd got an out-of-character helpful push from Dale Earnhardt. Photo/Bob Brodbeck.

Sterling Marlin had six top fives and no wins. Photo/Taylors Photography.

Geoff Bodine won once, placing sixth in points. Photo/Stan Clinton.

Most exciting finish: Rusty Wallace chasing Ricky Rudd to the line on the Watkins Glen road course.

Wallace, the tour's best road racer, was behind Rudd, likely the second best. Throughout the last lap, Wallace nudged at Rudd's rear bumper, trying to force an error. Rudd resolutely held the line. In the final right-hander, Wallace drove his Pontiac across Rudd's stern, off the blacktop and into the grass, barely avoiding the rail. Great stuff, Bobby. Rudd's victory was the first for car owner Kenny Bernstein.

Most terrifying crash: Richard Petty's car-shredding roll off Turn Four at Daytona.

Relatively few saw your wreck, Bobby. It's hard to see that turn from the Pocono grandstand. And the TV cameras missed it entirely. Petty's roll, on the other hand, was live on CBS and may have been the single most replayed piece of tape in all of television for the year. He was lucky and got out with nothing worse than a sore ankle.

Worst recurring snafu: NASCAR's handling of its pace cars.

On at least two occasions, pace cars picked up the wrong car as leader of a race. And once, the pace car went onto a track when there was no caution flag. In each case, officials said resulting scoring problems were corrected, but there were an awful lot of fans and competitors who remained unconvinced.

Easiest pickings: Grand National races won by Winston Cup drivers dropping down a class.

Winston Cup regulars—with better cars, better engines, better pit crews, bigger sponsors, and apparently unlimited greed—won 14 of the 30 Grand National races in 1988.

It's as if Danny Sullivan and Mario Andretti made a habit of putting down the youngsters in the American Racing Series. Or Alain Prost and Ayrton Senna decided to get fat dominating Formula Three.

Winston Cup drivers can say what they like about doing it for extra track time, or for the enjoyment their crews get, or because promoters want the big names at GN races—it still reeks.

Ken Schrader goes through (or under) the wringer happily while cooling off after his first-ever Winston Cup victory in the Talladega 500. Beneath a blisteringly hot Alabama sun, Schrader went from fourth to first on the final lap to win the prestigious affair. Photo/Brian McLeod.

Fans were still leaving the stands at Richmond in February when the old Richmond began to succumb to the bulldozer. A new super-duper Richmond resurfaced six months later. Photo/Ken Brown-Competition Photographers.

This encounter with the wall put an end to Dave Marcis' Budweiser 500 race at Dover. Photo/Tom Bernhardt.

Rusty Wallace's crew performed flawlessly all year. His engine man, David Evans, won the $20,000 Engine Builder of the Year Award, and Jimmy Makar accepted the $20,000 Mechanic of the Year Award. "I'm happy with all we accomplished this year," said Rusty, "but I'd be lying if I said we weren't disappointed in not winning the Winston Cup championship. We will be back in 1989. . . ." Photo/Jim Harris.

Brett Bodine (#15) stays low to let brother Geoff (#5) and Terry Labonte draft by at the Atlanta Journal 500. Photo/Sidell Tilghman.

Funniest new nickname since Cale Yarborough called Darrell Waltrip "Jaws": "Conehead"—coined by Wallace for Geoff Bodine after Bodine plowed into him under caution in the opening moments of the September race in Richmond.

Wallace, eliminated from the race by the crash, declared that if he lost the championship it would be Bodine's fault. Wallace's 35th-place finish was his worst of the season—by 10 positions.

Best facelift: The six-month metamorphosis of the frumpy half-mile Richmond Fairgrounds Raceway oval into the sassy, 3/4-mile tri-oval Richmond International Raceway.

Most significant team change for 1989: Engine builder Lou LaRosa's defection from Earnhardt's team to Rudd's.

This is a tough category, Bobby. Junior Johnson's switch from Chevy to Ford ranks high, as does Team Manager Harry Hyde's departure from Rick Hendrick's stable, where he had rediscovered his winning touch. He'll run Bobby Hillin's team in '89.

But LaRosa's jump has deeper implications (despite Earnhardt's graceless remark that a janitor's decision to quit the team that same week was more important). LaRosa was engine builder for all three of Earnhardt's championships, and his decision to leave is the first major change in that team since 1986.

Rudd, who lost excellent chances to win at least half-a-dozen races because of engine failures, becomes an instant title contender.

Most refreshing new winner: Alan Kulwicki, who took a wrong-way "Polish victory lap" after his win at Phoenix.

Other new winners were Lake Speed (Darlington spring race), Phil Parsons (Talladega spring race) and Ken Schrader (Talladega summer race). Parsons and Schrader may both be waking in the dead of night in a cold sweat, repeating the names of Richard Brickhouse, Dick Brooks, Lennie Pond, and Ron Bouchards—all Talladega one-win wonders.

Easiest race story angle: No question, Bobby—your narrow victory over your son, Davey, in the Daytona 500.

A blown tire in practice at Watkins Glen didn't deter Phil Parsons from putting on a great race. He led six of the 90 laps and took a fourth behind Rudd, Wallace and Elliott. Photo/Stan Clinton.

Odd to think you might need to be refreshed on Davey's career. He joined the circuit full-time in 1987 and has run like a rocket ever since. He has won four races, two in 1988, and is the leader of the latest youth movement.

As for the old guard, you had been holding the fort alone. When you out-thought and out-drove Davey and streaked under the checkered a car length ahead, you extended your oldest-winner-in-tour-history record another year to age 50.

Dale Jarrett (#29), Dave Marcis (#71) and Neil Bonnett (#75) go three abreast at Dover. Bonnett won two in a row early on, then leveled off to end up 16th for the year. Photo/Tom Bernhardt.

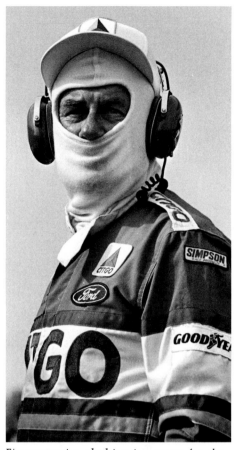

Terry Labonte's car owner and longtime Chevy man Junior Johnson, reportedly fed up with Chevrolet over team loyalties, announced he'd move over to Ford for '89. Photo/Al Steinberg.

Fire-protective clothing is a must for the fuel-handlers in the pits! Photo/Jim Harris.

When his engine popped at the early Atlanta race, Foyt had to eat some smoke before he brought his Copenhagen Olds to its final rest. Photo/Al Steinberg.

Veteran crew chief Waddell Wilson turned the wrenches for Geoff Bodine, who drove one of the three Monte Carlos fielded by well-known Charlotte, North Carolina, car dealer Rick Hendrick. Photo/Brian McLeod.

Although Dale Earnhardt failed to win a third straight championship, there were some happy times for the Richard Childress-owned Goodwrench Racing Team. Cecil Gordon (l.) and Childress celebrate a victory at Martinsville. Photo/Brian McLeod.

Your generation of superstars has just about had it. Richard Petty hasn't won a race since July, 1984. An awful lot of people watch him struggling to regain his winning touch and wonder if he ought to pack it in.

Cale Yarborough called it quits at the end of this year after three seasons without winning anything (and yielded to you in the long-running battle for third place on the all-time Winston Cup victory list, retiring with 83 wins to your 84). He'll be a gentleman car owner now. Likewise, Buddy Baker retired from driving to manage his own team. Benny Parsons decided to become a full-time broadcaster. David Pearson hasn't raced in a couple of years.

Just as your success may have inspired some of these guys to keep going, so the reality of your accident may have brought into focus the reasons to retire.

From the moment you were hurt, news of your condition overshadowed the tour itself. Even the slightest improvements were greeted with hope and relief.

At the track, every team—and it seemed nearly every fan—sported the slogan, "Hurry Back Bobby."

At first we heard that you were "out of it" for hours at a time. But reports began to filter down from friends and relatives that your lucid periods were getting longer, and that you were beginning to sound like the Bobby we knew—wisecracking and contentious, interested in things.

At the September race in Richmond, a long distance telephone hookup with the public address system allowed you to give the command to start the engines. Caught by surprise, the crowd erupted with a roar of relief and delight and thanksgiving, drowning the sound of 36 growling motors.

Alan Kulwicki's crew dumped a splash of fuel into his Zerex Ford at Dover. Our reporter calls him the "most refreshing new winner" of the year, for taking a wrong-way "Polish victory lap" after his win at Phoenix. Photo/Ken Brown-Competition Photographers.

Darrell Waltrip leads a hungry pack in his Tide Chevrolet. Chevy's General Manager, Bob Burger, accepted an unprecedented sixth consecutive Winston Cup manufacturers championship at the NASCAR awards banquet in December. In '89 the Monte Carlo SS will be parked in favor of the new Lumina coupe.
Photo/Steve Swope.

Lake Speed, spinning at Richmond, joined an elite group of first-time winners by taking the checkered flag at Darlington. The '88 season boasted the most first-time winners in one year, four—a modern day record.
Photo/Ken Brown-Competition Photographers.

The field gets a send-off from the chief starter at Atlanta's season finale. Winston Cup competitors raced for total posted awards of $16.7 million in 1988. The sport continues to grow in popularity with spectator attendance up and an all-time record crowd witnessing the final race at Riverside! Photo/Sidell Tilghman.

As testimony to the importance of seat belts—both on the highway and the race track—the STP Pontiac Richard Petty demolished in the Daytona 500, was put on display to encourage their use. Petty was unhurt. Photo/Jim Harris.

Proud daddy Darrell Waltrip shows off his progeny, Jessica Leigh, to another big daddy— Richard Petty. Photo/Tom Riles.

A month later, you showed up in person at Charlotte. The speculation turned to whether or not you will race again. Your doctors didn't rule out a return to the tour. You said if you heal enough, you want to do it.

Before you decide, Bobby, you should understand something. Whether you regain the memory of your whole career, or you need to consult the record books to fill in the gaps, the numbers only begin to tell your story. If you want to judge what you have meant to the sport, there is a measure more certain than any statistic.

You will find that measure in the respect your peers accord you. You will find it in the genuine affection of the fans who willed your recovery from their hearts, who cheered madly at the sound of your voice as it said, "Gentlemen, start your. . ."

You have already given them all they really wanted when they urged you to "Hurry Back." You escaped the grip of their darkest fear. For them, and for you, there can be nothing left to prove.

After narrowly losing to him, Davey Allison graciously shared the victory circle with father Bobby at the Daytona 500. Four months after his terrifying crash, Bobby finally showed up in person at Charlotte. The speculation turned to whether or not he would race again. Bobby said if he healed enough he would. Photo/Tom Riles.

Such hams these winners are. At Phoenix, Alan Kulwicki called "time out" to spruce up his looks before he'd grant ESPN an interview following his first Winston Cup win. Photo/Taylors Photography.

Benny's little brother, Phil, winner at Alabama International Speedway in May. Phil placed ninth in points in his Crown Olds. Photo/Ken Brown-Competition Photographers.

Ricky Rudd was a key player in our reporter's "most exciting finish." On the last lap on the Watkins Glen road course, push came to shove as Wallace, "drove his Pontiac across Rudd's stern, off the blacktop and into the grass, barely avoiding the rail." Rudd's win was the first for car owner Kenny Bernstein. Photo/Bruce R. Schulman.

Taking over for Bobby Allison, Mike Alexander compromised his chances to win the Grand National title by attempting to compete in both series. Photo/Werner Fritz.

A.J. Foyt, a true legend, ran seven Winston Cup races in '88. Photo/Jim Harris.

Ready to quit in '87 after breaking his thighbone in a crash, Neil Bonnett returned to win two races. Photo/Taylors Photography.

Kyle Petty scored no wins, and finished in the top five only twice. Photo/Ken Brown-Competition Photographers.

NASCAR/Busch Grand National

by AL PEARCE

***T**HE RECORD WILL SHOW* that Tommy Ellis clinched NASCAR's '88 Grand National championship with his ninth-place finish in a late-October race at Rockingham, North Carolina. Mike Alexander's 17th-place finish that Saturday afternoon officially erased him from contention, 29 races after the season opened in Daytona Beach.

The record is wrong. Realistically, the championship was decided on June 19 when Bobby Allison was injured in a Winston Cup race at Pocono. Two days later, Busch Series leader Alexander virtually forfeited the title by agreeing to drive Allison's car the rest of the Winston Cup season. At the same time, he vowed to keep chasing the Grand National title.

Tommy Ellis (driving #99) rose from the ashes of what he thought was an ended career to capture the second-biggest prize in stock car racing in 1988, the NASCAR Busch Grand National Series championship. Photo/Tom Bernhardt.

The grind of running two NASCAR series quickly beat him down. He went from 99 points ahead of Ellis to seven behind in just three races, a deficit he never made up. He eventually fell 136 points behind, got within eight late in the season, then lost his shot when Ellis beat him in five of the last six races.

The punch that kayoed Alexander in October was launched much earlier. On June 24-26, for example, he dashed between Louisville and Jackson, Michigan, for Busch Series and Winston Cup races. He ran at both Daytona Beach and Myrtle Beach on July 2; commuted between Pennsylvania and Virginia for a double-header July 17-19; ran an Alabama-Virginia double-header July 29-31; then jetted between a Virginia short track and Watkins Glen the second weekend in August.

Tommy Houston was a bit shaken at Darlington after he collided with the pace car following the race. Houston won three times in '88 and placed fifth in points. Photo/Jim Harris.

Defending champion, Larry Pearson (l.), with dad and former Winston Cup racer David, won the season-long Busch Pole Award with five poles and ended up fourth in points. He'll move into Winston Cup in '89. Photo/Jim Harris.

"I needed more track time," Alexander said after stumbling badly and finishing behind Ellis and runner-up Robbie Moroso in the final standings. "The crew worked hard and I drove hard, but yes, running both series affected me. I just couldn't spend enough time with the Busch car. Winston Cup racing is where I want to be, so driving Bobby's car was something I couldn't turn down. I won't second-guess my decisions. Tommy ran strong all year; he earned it."

Ellis' championship becomes more impressive when you realize he didn't even have a ride until December of '87. That's when New York businessmen John Jackson and Bill Papke agreed that Ellis could use their equipment and checkbook to chase the '88 title from his shop in Richmond. They had sponsored Merv

Treichler for part of the '87 season, then backed Ellis for a few races after Treichler quit at mid-season. The men were impressed enough to give Ellis their blessing.

Given the champ's hands-on, no-nonsense, kick-butt approach to racing, they were wise to stand aside. Although his take-no-prisoners attitude has made enemies along the way, nobody's ever questioned Tommy Ellis' ability to prepare and drive a race car. He loitered near the top in points through the spring and early summer before taking the lead for good at South Boston, Virginia, on July 23. He won twice at Hampton, Virginia, and once at Louisville, and finished among the top 10 in 20 of the year's 30 races. Week-in and week-out, this "rookie" team was the one to beat.

Mike Alexander virtually forfeited the title by agreeing to drive Bobby Allison's Winston Cup car after Bobby was injured at Pocono. At the same time, he vowed to keep chasing the Grand National title, but fell short, ending up third. Photo/Jim Harris.

Larry Pearson's '88 season got off to a rough start at Daytona. Runner-up in points Rob Moroso (#25) stayed clear of the spinning Pearson. Photo/Howard Hodge.

"I needed more track time," Mike Alexander (l.) said after leading early on then stumbling badly and finishing third in points. "The crew worked hard and I drove hard, but yes, running both series affected me." Photo/Jim Harris.

And what of Ellis' most serious challengers? Well, second-place Moroso (yes, that Moroso) won a short-track and superspeedway race and led the tour in money won. Third-place Alexander won a short track race early in the year, then steadily slipped backward after getting Allison's ride. Nineteen-eighty-six and '87 champ Larry Pearson won three times, but didn't have the consistent OOMPH! needed for a third title. Tommy Houston (three wins), Rick Mast (two), and Jimmy Hensley (one), weren't strong enough often enough to unseat Ellis. Rough-and-tumble newcomer Jimmy Spencer didn't make many friends enroute to a seventh place in points. And not much was heard from former series' champs L.D. Ottinger and Jack Ingram.

The leading race winner in '88 was Harry Gant in the Skoal Bandit Buick, who won five of the last seven events. Here, he aims for Rob Moroso (#25), the series' youngest two-time winner at 19. Photo/Howard Hodge.

Perky Patty Moise made some Grand National appearances in '88, in her Crisco Butter-Flavor Buick. Here, she takes to the low side at Dover Downs, as Elton Sawyer (#42) and Tommy Houston (#6) stay high. Photo/Howard Hodge.

Much was heard (too much, some said) from the Winston Cup drivers who took $550,000 from the Busch Series and won 14 races: five by Harry Gant and one each by Bobby Allison, Mark Martin, Geoff Bodine, Dale Earnhardt, Darrell Waltrip, Dale Jarrett, Bobby Hillin, Morgan Shepherd, and Mike Waltrip. More often than not, they dominated the top five in each of the 10 superspeedway races.

What does the future hold for the Grand National tour? Alexander and Pearson are moving on to full-time Winston Cup rides. Moroso and Spencer have stamped themselves as championship contenders, causing vets like Ellis, Houston, Mast, Ottinger, and Ingram to look over their shoulders. And struggling youngsters like Ed Berrier, Billy Standridge, Steve Grissom, Ronald Cooper and Elton Sawyer will have to keep paying their dues.

After all, the more this series changes, the more it remains the same.

It was a battle for the lead at Martinsville among (l. to r.) Geoff Bodine, Tommy Houston and Tommy Ellis in the Winston Classic. Harry Gant, in the Skoal Bandit, however, squeaked by this front pack to take the win. Photo/Howard Hodge.

Larry Pearson's Chevy sported a crinkled fender in the Pennsylvania 300 at Nazareth Speedway. Photo/Tom Bernhardt.

Rough-and-tumble newcomer Jimmy Spencer (#34) didn't make many friends en route to a seventh place in points. Here, he leads Mark Martin, Jack Ingram and Joe Milliken.
Photo/Howard Hodge.

At Darlington in September, Davey Allison got quick pit action. Davey drove a Buick in the Grand National series to give his sponsor, Havoline more visibility. Photo/Jim Harris.

Surprisingly, Brad Teague missed the wall while spinning twice on the backstretch at Rockingham. Photo/Dick Conway.

Tommy Ellis, the 1988 Busch Grand National champion. Photo/Dick Conway.

Bristol took its toll in April on Rob Moroso (#25), Brad Teague (#75), Larry Pearson (#21), Jimmy Hensley (#5) and Larry Pollard (#00). Photo/Dick Conway.

NASCAR/Busch Grand National North

by **MIKE ROWELL**

NASCAR *NORTH FLOURISHED* in its third year, attracting new racers and big crowds. One of these new racers was Dale Shaw of Center Conway, New Hampshire, who joined the Tour in the middle of the '87 season. Shaw entered the '88 season loaded for bear. Since North Tour drivers can add points from two Southern Tour races to their points total, Shaw ran in four races in the South before the season-opener at Monadnock in Keene, New Hampshire.

Kelly Moore, of Scarborough, Maine, immediately challenged Shaw's points lead and the two battled throughout the 16-race season. Moore was very fast, winning two races and nine pole positions; but Dale Shaw was more consistent with 11 top-five finishes to Moore's seven. Significantly, in many races Shaw finished just the one or two positions ahead of Moore necessary to hold his slim points lead.

The Busch Grand National North top three enjoy the sponsor's product: (from l.) Dick McCabe, series runner-up, the champ Jamie Aube, and third-place finisher Dale Shaw. Photo/Howard Hodge.

Jamie Aube of North Ferrisburg, Vermont, in his first year on the tour, became the 1988 Grand National North champion. Photo/Howard Hodge.

After winning the biggest race of the year, the Oxford 250, Dick McCabe's crew rewarded him with an ice water shower. Photo/Howard Hodge.

But these two were not the only racers. Jamie Aubie of North Ferrisburg, Vermont, was in his first year on the North Tour, but he is a highly experienced driver. He won one of the races at Jenerstown, Pennsylvania, and wracked up a number of seconds and thirds. Then, with just three races left in the season, with Dale Shaw's team tiring and Moore's team running into bad luck, Aubie jumped from third to first in points.

Twenty-five-year-veteran Dick McCabe was also moving up in points, winning the Oxford 250 and another Oxford race to pass Shaw. In the season finale at Epping, New Hampshire, Shaw placed second and McCabe third, but it was not enough. The final points race went to Aubie with McCabe second and Shaw third.

Twenty-five-year-veteran Dick McCabe won two races to place second behind Jamie Aube. Photo/Howard Hodge.

Kelly Moore (#47) challenged Dale Shaw's (#60) early-season points lead, and the two battled throughout the 16-race season. Moore was very fast, winning two races and nine pole positions, but ended up fifth. Photo/Howard Hodge.

IROC

Al Unser, Jr. (r.) earned his second IROC championship by winning the final IROC race at Watkins Glen. In IROC's 12-year history, only Foyt (1976 and '77) and Unser, Jr. (1986 and '88) have won the title twice. "Little Al" also tied for second place in IROC history with four race wins. His dad, Al Sr. (l.) ended up eighth. Photo/Art Flores.

IROC XII featured a dozen of the world's finest racing drivers competing for $750,000 in identically-prepared Camaros at four premier U.S. racing circuits— Daytona, Riverside, Michigan and Watkins Glen. Photo/Tom Riles.

Al Holbert was seventh in points. Photo/Bill Stahl.

Winston Cup racer Terry Labonte was runner-up to Al Jr. Photo/Bill Stahl.

The Daytona opener and a fourth for the series went to Bill Elliott. Photo/Art Flores.

Scott Pruett won at Riverside, taking third in points. Photo/Randy McKee.

The IROC series was first run in 1973, using equally-prepared Porsche Carreras. In 1974 a switch was made to Chevrolet Camaros, and to the IROC-Z model in 1985. Photo/Taylors Photography.

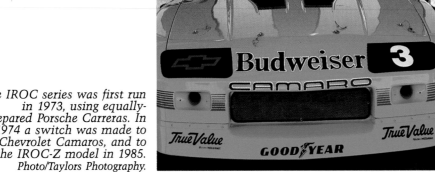

In just three IROC series, Unser, Jr. has pocketed $470,400, easily out-distancing previous series record holder Cale Yarborough's total of $313,000 in eight IROC appearances. Photo/Steve Swope.

IROC

The IROC series is not without a few nudges. Here, Pruett and defending champion Geoff Bodine go at it at Watkins Glen. Pruett finished third, Bodine went off course, damaging his Camaro too severely to continue. Photo/Stan Clinton.

Bill Elliott proved that ovals were like an old pair of slippers to him by winning the first IROC race of the season on the high banks of Daytona. Photo/Al Steinberg.

IROC's top two, Al Jr. and Terry Labonte, ran close at Michigan. Photo/Steve Swope.

Winston Cup champ Dale Earnhardt had the edge over Al Jr. at Michigan, taking a second behind Geoff Bodine, but ended up fifth in points. Photo/Steve Swope.

Large crowds were treated to racing by America's best, among drivers Geoff Bodine, Chris Cord, Dale Earnhardt, Bill Elliott, Roberto Guerrero, Al Holbert, Terry Labonte, Scott Pruett, Bobby Rahal, Chip Robinson, Al Unser and Al Unser, Jr. Photo/Steve Swope.

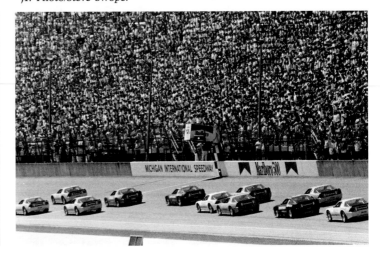

SCORE-HDRA-MTEG/Off-Road

by JEAN CALVIN
PUBLISHER, *DUSTY TIMES*

OFF-ROAD RACING MADE substantial gains in recognition in 1988, with ever-increasing manufacturer interest in both the desert series and the stadium contests. It also suffered tragic losses of pioneers in the sport. First, on March 16, came the brutal murders of Mickey and Trudy Thompson, gunned down early in the morning as they were leaving their home for the offices of the Mickey Thompson Entertainment Group (MTEG). Then, on July 2, during the Fireworks 250 at Barstow, California, HDRA President and founder Walt Lott suffered a fatal heart attack. These people and their leadership can never be forgotten and a credit to them is that both organizations have carried on without missing a beat.

In the SCORE-HDRA Desert Series the entry numbers were up in almost all of the eight events. More major manufacturers jumped on the sponsorship and contingency prize donor bandwagon, enriching, in particular, the seven classes of various size trucks, from bone-stock minis to highly modified V8-powered chargers. Still, the bulk of the entry continued to be in the open wheel and Baja Bug categories; with the limited 1600 engine, the limited engine and chassis Challenger classes producing well over 50 starters each in several events.

The desert events take place in Arizona, California, Nevada, and Baja California, Mexico. Each race course has unique qualities and varied terrain. The weather can be in the three digits or cold enough to snow. Off-road racers must prepare for cold to hot, rain, sometimes snow, or maybe bright sunshine, in almost every instance.

The overall Desert Series points champion came, again this year, from the Challenger Class of open wheel cars. Nick Gross and Joe Valentine earned the honor by winning the huge class at three events and never placing worse than fifth. The Mini Metal Championship went to Mike Lesle, the Class 7 4x4 points winner, who also won the class in '87, both years driving a Jeep Comanche.

The sensation of the desert this year was 19-year-old Robby Gordon, who switched from his father's Class 2 open-wheeler to a privately sponsored Ford V8 pickup. Robby proceeded to win three races in Class 8, place high in the others, winning the class points and the overall Heavy Metal Championship by one single point. Robby was honored by the vote of his peers as the 1988 Driver of the Year. His father, Bob Gordon, was the Class 2 points winner, and the Toyota True Grit winner for the fastest average speed of the year while finishing all eight events. The Gordon trophy shelf is overflowing.

The overall Desert Series points champion came, again this year, from the Challenger Class of open-wheel cars. Nick Gross and Joe Valentine earned the honor by winning the huge class at three events and never placing worse than fifth. Photo/Trackside Photo.

Whoopeeee! Bob Richey took a flying leap and landed in fifth place in Class 2 season points. Photo/J.C. Taylor.

Hartmut and Wolfram Klawitter romped to the Class 5 Unlimited Baja Bug title in a state-of-the-art racer. Photo/Trackside Photo.

Mark McMillin won the Class 1 single-seat unlimited points title for the third year in a row, winning four of the eight events in class, a couple overall. Mark became the first off-road racer to go to Germany for the Porsche Cup awards, using a 3-liter, 6-cylinder Porsche engine in his Chenowth. Gary Cogbill and John Marking won top honors in the biggest entry class, 1-2-1600, with one win and consistent high placings. The other open wheel class, 10, features 1650cc engines and no other restrictions. Small water-cooled engines are the rage in this class, but Michael Church won the points using the tried-and-true VW air-cooled engine.

Mini truck class entries are growing monthly. For the modified units in Class 7S, the usual winner, Ford, was usurped in 1988. Larry Ragland drove a Chevy S-10 to the championship with three wins. The stock 2WD class points went to the Ford Ranger of Paul Simon in a tight battle. The Class 5 Unlimited Baja Bug title went to Hartmut and Wolfram Klawitter in a state-of-the-art race car. Andy DeVercelly repeated his 1987 championship in the 1600 limited chassis Bugs. Mexico's Ramon Castro won the stock VW class for the third year in a row.

The big 4x4s have three classes. Mike Schwellinger repeated his 1987 title in Class 3 driving a Jeep CJ-7, while Jack Johnson won Class 4 in a modified Nissan. In the "run what you brung 4x4" Class 14, Boone England took top points driving a tame looking Chevy Blazer. The Moser brothers, Greg, Wes and G.W., drove a Ford Ranchero to the Class 6 title in the class featuring older cars.

In the MTEG Stadium Series, featuring three classes for four-wheel racers, the name Robby Gordon pops up again. The teenager won many of the Stadium Series events in Super 1650cc competition in a Chenowth, winning the eight-race series championship on points. This class is similar to desert Class 12 in restrictions, but other than a similarity in appearance, the cars are set up quite differently.

Toyota won the Manufacturers Cup for the sixth year in a row on points in the Grand National Truck Stadium Class, and Toyota driver Steve Millen won the drivers points title again in 1988. The UltraStock Class, tube-frame cars with auto-style bodies, saw Jeff Elrod win top honors in a Volkswagen-bodied Mirage. The eight-race series played in stadiums from Seattle to San Diego, and from Los Angeles to Texas during 1988. It will expand to 10 events and to New Orleans in 1989.

The media exposure for off-road racing grew considerably in 1988, with ESPN doing one hour shows on all eight desert events. There were 10 TV shows featuring the MTEG Stadium Series. This exposure may be the trigger that is igniting so much sponsor interest in these two very different forms of the sport. But both are now firmly in the big leagues of auto racing, and the future looks bright.

The sensation of the desert was Robby Gordon of Orange, California, who at just 19, captured the Overall Heavy-Metal championship driving a Ford pickup truck in Class 8. He was voted Driver of the Year, the youngest to ever win the award. Photo/Trackside Photo.

In his Porsche-powered Chenowth, Mark McMillin sped to the Class 1 single-seat unlimited points title for the third year in a row, winning four of eight events. Mark became the first off-road racer to go to Stuttgart for the Porsche Cup awards. Photo/Trackside Photo.

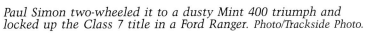

Paul Simon two-wheeled it to a dusty Mint 400 triumph and locked up the Class 7 title in a Ford Ranger. Photo/Trackside Photo.

In Class 5-1600 limited chassis Bugs, it was Andy L. DeVercelly once again. Photo/Trackside Photo.

Mike Lesle not only won Class 7 4x4 in a Jeep Comanche, but added a third HDRA/SCORE driving championship to his impressive list of accomplishments. Photo/Trackside Photo.

Larry Ragland leaps a cattle guard at Baja in his Chevy S-10 to grab the Class 7S championship for mini-trucks. Photo/Trackside Photo.

Bob Gordon wasn't bogged down for long, as he popped out of the dirt to take the Class 2 championship. Father of rising star Robby, Bob was also the Toyota True Grit winner for the fastest average speed of the year while finishing all eight events! Photo/Trackside Photo.

Finland's Ari Vatanen heads for the 14,110-ft. summit of Pikes Peak in his ultra-high-tech Peugeot 405 Turbo 16. Snow and sleet on the top third of the course caused times to be slower than expected, but Vatanen was still able to set a new overall record as well as an Open Rally division record for the hill. He bested Walter Roehrl's record time, set in 1987 in an Audi S1 Quattro, by just .63 of a second! Photo/Su Kemper.

Local Colorado Springs resident, Ralph Bruning, was the winner in the Stock Car division in a Buick. This was his sixth win at the Peak. Photo/Sidell Tilghman.

Pikes Peak

Roger Mears, in a new Nissan Hardbody stadium truck, dominated the truck class during the first two days of practice. The truck was later put into the "Unlimited" class for having too large an engine and Roger ultimately blew that engine on race day. Photo/Sidell Tilghman.

Clive Smith, a transplanted New Zealander and off-road racer, won Class 7 for desert trucks in this quick Chevy S10. He missed the overall truck title by being just six seconds slower than Glenn Harris. Photo/Trackside Photo.

Stadium truck racer Glenn Harris became the only driver to ever set two records in one day at the Peak. He first won the Rally Group A class in a Mazda 323 4WD, then helicoptered back to the starting line to clinch the overall "Fastest Truck" title in his Mazda B-2600 pickup. Photo/Trackside Photo.

Robby Unser, youngest son of racing great Bobby, made a most successful debut in the Open Wheel division this year by setting a new record in his Jones Intercable Special. Photo/Su Kemper.

SCCA/Pro Rally Series

by SU KEMPER

WITH THE ABSENCE OF 10-time U.S. Pro Rally champion John Buffum, now serving as SCCA series steward, the 1988 title looked to be an easy grab for Rod Millen. The New Zealand transplant, now living in California, had been at John's heels for some years now, proving himself world-class material. But a couple of young lions nearly upset the applecart—or the Mazda in Rodney's case—and provided more excitement than anyone really anticipated.

Of chief concern was a Buffum-clone, specifically JB's own step-son, Paul Choiniere. Driving an Audi Coupe Quattro, "Thumper" (as tagged by his rivals) competed in five events and won three outright. Chad DiMarco, at the wheel of a 4WD Subaru three-door Coupe was also a threat. He won the Happy Trails Rally in Washington state, plus several top-five placings elsewhere.

Millen trailed both his rivals going into the penultimate event, the notorious Press On Regardless in Michigan. A bad choice of tires put him at a serious disadvantage, and Choiniere quickly took command. DiMarco failed to finish, and took himself out of the running for the championship. Then, to Millen's dismay, the final event on the schedule was cancelled. But his luck turned favorable, and there was a replacement rally to give him the one chance he needed.

The standings showed Choiniere with a 14-point advantage over the Kiwi going into this final round. Millen ran a conservative rally, winning it by a sizeable 12 + minute margin while Choiniere made a bad judgement call and found himself irretrievably mired off the road in mud and out of the chase for good. The win gave Millen the overall championship by six points over Choiniere while he also collected the Group A title by an identical points spread over DiMarco.

In the Production class, it was a two-man race throughout the season with defending class champ Guy Light (VW GTI 16v) trying desperately to hold off the ever increasing advances of Canadian rallyist Niall Leslie in a Toyota Corolla GTS. The two teams were incredibly alike. All season they chased each other, setting stage times only one or two seconds apart with the final results usually being within 10 seconds of each other. But it was Leslie who clinched the championship at the P.O.R. when Light failed to finish due to electrical problems. These two drivers were great entertainment and provided the most exciting duels we've seen in the sport in many years. Finally tally: Leslie—142, Light—115.

Rod Millen, the 1988 Pro Rally champion, is more than just a driver. He oversees all facets of his Newport Racing rally effort. Photo/Gerald Schallie.

Rod Millen clawed his way to the top in his Mazda 323 GTX by finally outdistancing his main rivals, Paul Choiniere and Chad DiMarco, at the final round. The win gave Millen the overall championship by six points over Choiniere, and he collected the Group A title by an identical points spread over DiMarco. Photo/Su Kemper.

A dismal showing of only 29 cars began the Olympus Rally in June. Miki (Massimo) Biasion of Italy, the eventual 1988 world rally champion, was the winner in a Lancia Delta Integrale. And it was at this event that Lancia clinched the world manufacturers crown, making it the earliest ever that a title fight had been decided. Photo/Gerald Schallie.

John Buffum, 1987 Pro Rally champ, drove his step-son's Audi Coupe Quattro in the Olympus Rally. Paul Choiniere, considered a Buffum clone, nearly snatched the title from Rod Millen, but electrical problems in the final event dashed his hopes. Photo/Su Kemper.

This season Doug Shepherd returned to form, driving a new Dodge Daytona, and handily won the GT class with five victories to his credit. The husband and wife team of Dan and Betty-Ann Gilliland, the '87 defending class champions, switched to a Dodge Shelby Shadow this year and won their class at one rally despite spending much of the season ironing out the bugs in the new car. The Gillilands were second for the year, 45 points behind Shepherd.

The Pro Rally Series was diminished this season by the loss of an active competitor, Jon Woodner, and of our premier rally, the Olympus world championship.

Woodner, who lived in Washington, D.C. and drove a Group B Peugeot 205 Turbo 16 rally car in American events, was killed in April while flying an experimental Formula One racing aircraft. Jon, a former road racer who moved into rallying in the late seventies, loved performance rallying and was well liked by everyone who knew him. His presence will be greatly missed.

Canadian rallyist Niall Leslie in a Toyota Corolla GTS clinched the Production class, but it was a two-man race between Leslie and defending class champ Guy Light throughout the season. Photo/Su Kemper.

Doug Shepherd returned to form this season, driving a new Dodge Daytona, and handily won the GT class with five victories to his credit. Photo/Gerald Schallie.

The Olympus Rally, the U.S. qualifying round to the world rally championship, took place as an unsponsored event last June, counting towards both the world drivers and manufacturers championships. With FISA dropping the 50-car starting requirement from its rules in 1988 the event was free to start whatever they could. A dismal showing of only 29 cars began the event. Miki (Massimo) Biasion of Italy, the eventual 1988 world rally champion, was the winner in a Lancia Delta Integrale. And it was at this event that Lancia clinched the manufacturers crown; making it the earliest-ever that a title fight had been decided.

The organizers applied to FISA for their 1989 date and everything was thought to be going smoothly. However, when the FISA Plenary Committee meetings took place in Paris in October, the rally found itself demoted from world championship status; having the dubious honor of being the first WRC to be removed from the calendar without its organizers asking to be withdrawn. Unfortunately, the Olympus Rally will not be back next year, not even as a national event. With the loss of this prestigious, world class rally, the sport in the U.S. has moved a step backwards.

Production class runner-up Guy Light, and navigator Jim Brandt, negotiate rolling terrain in their VW GTI 16-Valve. Photo/Gerald Schallie.

Bill Holmes and Jim Rogers in their Ford F-150 pickup overcame three flat tires and a broken steering pump to lead the National group in the Wild West Rally, run concurrently with the Olympus. Photo/Gerald Schallie.

Track Profiles/1988

Alabama International Motor Speedway

Talladega, Alabama
2.66-mile, 33º-banked tri-oval

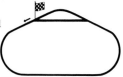

Atlanta International Raceway

Hampton, Georgia
1.522-mile oval with turns
banked 24º

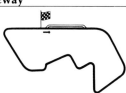

Brainerd International Raceway

Brainerd, Minnesota
3.0-mile, 10 turn road course

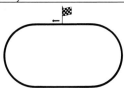

Burke Lakefront Airport

Cleveland, Ohio
2.48-mile, 12 turn
road course

Charlotte Motor Speedway

Charlotte, North Carolina
1.5-mile tri-oval with turns
banked 24º to 26º
2.25-mile, 12 turn
road course

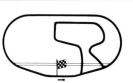

Columbus Grand Prix

Columbus, Ohio
2.67-mile, 11 turn road course

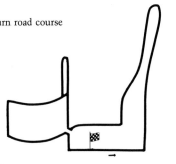

Dallas Grand Prix

Dallas, Texas
1.2-mile, 9 turn
road course

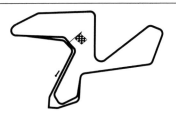

Darlington International Raceway

Darlington, South Carolina
1.366-mile oval with turns
banked 22º and 24º

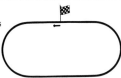

Daytona International Speedway

Daytona Beach, Florida
2.5-mile, 31º-banked tri-oval
3.84-mile, 12 turn
road course

Del Mar Fairgrounds

Del Mar, California
1.6-mile, 11 turn
road course

Detroit Grand Prix Circuit

Detroit, Michigan
2.59-mile, 16 turn road course

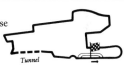

Indianapolis Motor Speedway

Speedway, Indiana
2.5-mile oval with turns
banked 9º

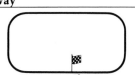

Laguna Seca Raceway

Monterey, California
1.9-mile, 9 turn road course
2.196-mile,
11 turn road course

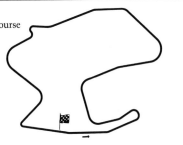

Lime Rock Park

Lime Rock, Connecticut
1.53-mile, 11 turn road course

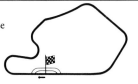

259

Long Beach Grand Prix Circuit

Long Beach, California
1.67-mile, 11 turn road course

Meadowlands Sports Complex

East Rutherford, New Jersey
1.2-mile, 6 turn road course

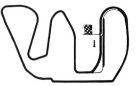

Memphis International Motorsports Park

Millington, Tennessee
1.78-mile,
11 turn
road course

Miami Grand Prix Circuit

Miami, Florida
1.87-mile, 12 turn
road course

Michigan International Speedway

Brooklyn, Michigan
2.0-mile oval with turns banked
1.9-mile, 9 turn road course

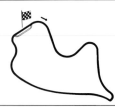

Mid-Ohio Sports Car Course

Lexington, Ohio
2.4-mile, 15 turn road course

Mosport Park

Durham Region, Ontario, Canada
2.459-mile, 10 turn road course

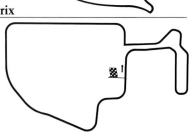

Niagara Falls Grand Prix

Niagara Falls, New York
1.75-mile,
11 turn road course

Pennsylvania International Raceway

Nazareth, Pennsylvania
1.0-mile, tri-oval

Phoenix International Raceway

Phoenix, Arizona
1.0-mile, semi-banked oval

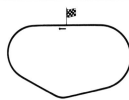

Pocono International Raceway

Long Pond, Pennsylvania
2.5-mile, tri-oval with turn 1
banked 16°, turn 2 banked 8°,
and turn 3 banked 6°.
2.5-mile, 9 turn road course

Road course runs clock-wise.

Portland International Raceway

Portland, Oregon
1.915-mile, 9 turn road course

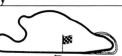

Riverside International Raceway

Riverside, California
2.62/3.3-mile, 9-turn
road course

Drag strip

Road America

Elkhart Lake, Wisconsin
4.0-mile, 11 turn road course

Road Atlanta

Braselton, Georgia
2.52-mile, 12 turn road course

Sanair Super Speedway

Quebec, Canada
1.33-kilometer, tri-oval

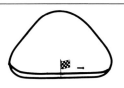

San Antonio Grand Prix

San Antonio, Texas
1.67-mile, 10 turn road course

Sears Point International Raceway

Sonoma, California
2.523-mile, 12 turn road course

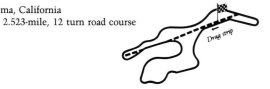

Sebring International Raceway

Sebring, Florida
4.11-mile, 13 turn road course

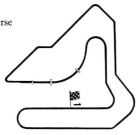

St. Petersburg Grand Prix

St. Petersburg, Florida
2.00-mile, 10 turn
road course

Summit Point Raceway

Summit Point, West Virginia
2.0-mile, 10 turn road course

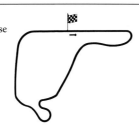

Tamiami Park

Miami, Florida
1.75-mile, 7 turn
road course

Tampa

Tampa, Florida
1.9-mile, 12 turn
road course

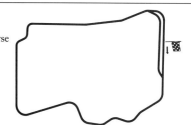

Toronto

Toronto, Ontario, Canada
1.78-mile, 11 turn
road course

Watkins Glen International

Watkins Glen, New York
3.377-mile, 11 turn road course
2.4-mile short course

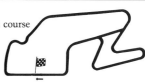

West Palm Beach

West Palm Beach, Florida
1.62-mile, 11 turn
road course

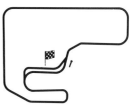

Wisconsin State Fair Park Speedway

Milwaukee, Wisconsin
1.0-mile oval with turns
banked 9°

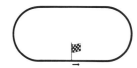

CART/PPG INDY CAR WORLD SERIES

DRIVER	POINTS	PHOENIX INT'L RACEWAY APRIL 10		LONG BEACH GRAND PRIX APRIL 17		WISCONSIN STATE FAIR PARK JUNE 5		PORTLAND INT'L RACEWAY JUNE 19		CLEVELAND GRAND PRIX JULY 3		TORONTO CANADA JULY 17		MEADOWLANDS GRAND PRIX JULY 24		MICHIGAN INT'L SPEEDWAY AUGUST 7		POCONO INT'L RACEWAY AUGUST 21		MID-OHIO SPORTS CAR COURSE SEPTEMBER 4		ROAD AMERICA SEPTEMBER 11	
		Q	F	Q	F	Q	F	Q	F	Q	F	Q	F	Q	F	Q	F	Q	F	Q	F	Q	F
1. Danny Sullivan	182	8	23*	1	13*	5	2	1	1	1	3	1	2	4	4	5	1	2	18*	1	5	1	4
2. Al Unser, Jr.	149	4	18*	4	1	4	20*	4	4	10	4	3	1	6	1	6	21*	11	2	2	4	3	7*
3. Bobby Rahal	136	12	16	8	2	7	6	6	12	4	2	5	5	10	5	4	2	3	1	3	18*	5	2
4. Rick Mears	129	1	22*	3	8	3	1	3	6	2	23*	8	6	5	3	1	13*	1	23*	5	3	2	12
5. Mario Andretti	126	3	1	2	15*	2	17*	5	5	3	1	2	25*	2	2*	3	12*	5	17*	4	2	6	3
6. Michael Andretti	119	10	3	5	7	1	7	8	11	7	14*	6	3	9	6	14	3	12	25*	7	26*	8	5
7. Emerson Fittipaldi	105	14	21*	7	16*	10	3	7	3	6	19*	4	4	1	14*	7	19*	8	21*	6	1	4	1
8. Raul Boesel	89	13	5	6	4	5	4	16	26*	11	5	9	8	7	9*	10	11*	9	5	26	6	11	14*
9. Derek Daly	53	15	13*	14	5	8	11	10	19*	9	6	7	23*	12	24*	8	16*	10	4	10	9	10	6
10. Teo Fabi	44	9	7	12	24	16	9	9	7	16	24*	10	10	3	18*	12	25*	25	24*	11	8	13	8
10. John Jones	44	19	20*	21	12*	17	14	15	8	14	7	13	7	19	7	26	8	24	8	13	7	15	13*

Q = Qualifying
F = Finished
* = Not running at the finish

NASCAR/BUSCH GRAND NATIONAL

DRIVER	POINTS	DAYTONA INT'L SPEEDWAY FEBRUARY 13		HICKORY SPEEDWAY FEBRUARY 28		NORTH CAROLINA MOTOR SPEEDWAY MARCH 5		MARTINSVILLE SPEEDWAY MARCH 13		DARLINGTON INT'L RACEWAY MARCH 26		BRISTOL INT'L RACEWAY APRIL 9		LANGLEY SPEEDWAY APRIL 30		PENNSYLVANIA INT'L RACEWAY MAY 7		SOUTH BOSTON SPEEDWAY MAY 14		NASHVILLE MOTOR RACEWAY MAY 21		CHARLOTTE MOTOR SPEEDWAY MAY 28	
		Q	F	Q	F	Q	F	Q	F	Q	F	Q	F	Q	F	Q	F	Q	F	Q	F	Q	F
1. Tommy Ellis	4310	15	18	2	4	3	6	8	22*	16	14	10	2	1	1	3	10	1	3	9	20*	8	12
2. Rob Moroso	4071	22	9	10	10	4	22	6	3	13	6	9	4	7	13	5	2	4	7	15	16	22	4
3. Mike Alexander	4053	26	7	9	1	12	2	21	4	18	11	6	13	9	9	1	18	2	2	10	9	3	9
4. Larry Pearson	4050	10	30*	3	6	5	35*	1	23*	21	7	1	14	2	2	14	22*	3	1	1	4	14	39*
5. Tommy Houston	4042	5	11	6	2	24	36*	9	11	37	16	3	7	12	4	11	19	8	5	11	7	37	25
6. Jimmy Hensley	3904	11	17	11	7	16	10	23	1	12	12	17	11	11	22	9	5	14	14	17	6	17	18
7. Jimmy Spencer	3839	8	29*	15	16	18	11	11	8	24	20	19	5	20	8	13	8	19	12	8	3	10	16
8. Rick Mast	3809	24	10	17	15	23	7	7	7	20	33*	15	9	4	11	12	1	11	10	3	13	11	21
9. L.D. Ottinger	3732	32	22*	16	14	13	30*	4	2	32	29*	14	17*	6	14	15	20*	5	6	13	10	28	15
10. Jack Ingram	3610	18	25*	12	3	7	23	17	5	23	25*	12	3	5	3	10	4	6	23*	2	2	35	19

NASCAR/BUSCH GRAND NATIONAL

DRIVER	DOVER DOWNS INT'L SPEEDWAY JUNE 4		ORANGE COUNTY SPEEDWAY JUNE 11		LANIER RACEWAY JUNE 19		LOUISVILLE MOTOR SPEEDWAY JUNE 25		MYRTLE BEACH SPEEDWAY JULY 2		OXFORD PLAINS SPEEDWAY JULY 10		SOUTH BOSTON SPEEDWAY JULY 16		HICKORY SPEEDWAY JULY 23		LANGLEY SPEEDWAY JULY 30		INDIANAPOLIS RACEWAY PARK AUGUST 6		ORANGE COUNTY SPEEDWAY AUGUST 13	
	Q	F	Q	F	Q	F	Q	F	Q	F	Q	F	Q	F	Q	F	Q	F	Q	F	Q	F
1. Tommy Ellis	4	6	6	6	6	17*	18	1	2	25*	17	7	20	2	17	3	1	1	14	3	8	7
2. Rob Moroso	3	12	14	4	9	18*	13	20*	4	1	15	40*	1	13	1	9	5	6	5	33*	12	3
3. Mike Alexander	1	10	2	5	3	5	4	4	9	20	13	43*	10	20	14	18*	3	8	20	11	4	2
4. Larry Pearson	2	2	23	2	1	3	11	19*	11	2	1	29*	3	6	6	5	2	7	29	4	1	21*
5. Tommy Houston	20	20	1	1	10	1	12	17*	10	3	27	38*	18	3	8	1	8	4	6	2	5	6
6. Jimmy Hensley	8	24*	11	7	4	2	7	3	6	15	11	28*	5	12	4	2	6	3	12	12	7	22*
7. Jimmy Spencer	10	28*	7	3	15	8	10	5	21	18	26	11	21	17	18	22*	21	9	22	17	15	16*
8. Rick Mast	11	23*	3	14	8	12	8	21*	5	6	25	13	7	5	15	8	9	5	19	18	2	1
9. L.D. Ottinger	6	11	12	9	14	4	2	2	1	21*	36	24	19	14	2	23*	7	13	10	13	14	5
10. Jack Ingram	7	25*	25	24	7	19*	21	22*	23	5	35	8	6	4	12	4	13	2	26	35*	21	11

Q = Qualifying
F = Finished
* = Not running at the finish

	PENNSYLVANIA INT'L RACEWAY SEPTEMBER 25		LAGUNA SECA RACEWAY OCTOBER 16		TAMIAMI PARK NOVEMBER 6	
	Q	F	Q	F	Q	F
	1	1	1	1	1	5
	6	19*	3	6	5	1
	5	12	4	4	9	18*
	2	7	7	5	4	2
	3	3	2	3	2	15*
	6	2	5	2	3	17*
	4	8	6	16*	6	20*
	7	5	11	21*	8	22*
	9	10	9	7	10	23*
	12	4	8	10	7	21*
	16	11	15	11*	14	16*

72nd INDIANAPOLIS 500

DRIVER	CAR	Q	F
Rick Mears	Pennzoil Z-7 Special/Penske Racing Penske PC17	1	1
Emerson Fittipaldi	Marlboro/Patrick Racing Team March 88C	8	2
Al Unser	Hertz/Penske Racing Penske PC17	3	3
Michael Andretti	Kraco Racing March 88C	10	4
Bobby Rahal	Budweiser/TrueSports Racing Lola T88/01	19	5
Jim Crawford	Mac Tools/King/Protofab/Kenny Bernstein Lola T87/01	18	6
Raul Boesel	Domino's Pizza/Team Shierson Lola T88/01	20	7
Phil Krueger	CNC Systems/Kent Baker Racing March 88C	15	8
Dick Simon	Uniden/Soundesign/Simon Racing Lola T88/00	16	9
Arie Luyendyk	Provimi Veal Racing Lola T88/01	6	10
Kevin Cogan	Schaefer/Playboy Fashion/Machinists Union March 88C	13	11
Howdy Holmes	Jiffy Mixes/Alex Morales Motorsports March 87C	33	12
Al Unser, Jr.	Team Valvoline/Galles Racing March 88C	5	13
Bill Vukovich III	Genesee Beer Wagon/Gohr Racing March 87C	23	14
Randy Lewis	Toshiba/Oracle/Altos/Leader Card Racing Lola T88/01	11	15
Rich Volger	Byrd's Cafeteria/Pepsi/Bryant March 87C	32	16*
Rocky Moran	Skoal/Trench Shoring/A.J. Foyt Enterprises March 88C	28	17*
Dominic Dobson	Moore Industries/Raynor Motorsports Group Lola T87/01	21	18*
Teo Palmroth	Bronson/Neste/Editor Racing Lola T87/01	25	19*
Mario Andretti	Amoco/K-Mart/Newman-Haas Racing Lola T87/01	4	20*
John Andretti	Skoal Bandit/Mike Curb Motorsports Lola T88/01	27	21*
Johnny Rutherford	Mac Tools/King/Protofab/Kenny Bernstein Lola T88/01	30	22*
Danny Sullivan	Miller High Life/Penske Racing Penske PC17	2	23*
Steve Chassey	Gary Trout Motorsports/Kaale Recycling Lola T87/01	26	24*
Ludwig Heimrath, Jr.	MacKenzie Ind. Group of Funds Lola T88/01	31	25*
A.J. Foyt	Copenhagen/Gilmore/Foyt Racing Lola T87/01	22	26*
Tom Sneva	Pizza Hut/WRTV Channel 6/Hemelgarn Racing Lola T87/01	14	27*
Teo Fabi	Quaker State/Porsche Motorsport N.A. March 88C	17	28*
Derek Daly	Raynor Motorsports Group Lola T88/01	9	29*
Stan Fox	Calumet Farm/Copenhagen/A.J. Foyt Ent. March 88C	29	30*
Scott Brayton	Amway/Lifecycle/Hemelgarn Racing Lola T88/01	7	31*
Roberto Guerrero	STP/Dianetics/Vince Granatelli Racing Lola T88/01	12	32*
Tony Bettenhausen	Hardee's/Bettenhausen Racing Association Lola T87/01	24	33*

Q = Qualifying
F = Finished
* = Not running at the finish

BRISTOL INT'L RACEWAY AUGUST 26		DARLINGTON INT'L RACEWAY SEPTEMBER 3		RICHMOND INT'L RACEWAY SEPTEMBER 10		DOVER DOWNS INT'L SPEEDWAY SEPTEMBER 17		MARTINSVILLE SPEEDWAY SEPTEMBER 24		CHARLOTTE MOTOR SPEEDWAY OCTOBER 8		NORTH CAROLINA MOTOR SPEEDWAY OCTOBER 22		MARTINSVILLE SPEEDWAY OCTOBER 30	
Q	F	Q	F	Q	F	Q	F	Q	F	Q	F	Q	F	Q	F
1	24*	15	14	28	4	16	2	1	15	27	6	19	9	3	3
6	27*	18	8	13	3	4	34*	3	10	13	1	12	11	5	2
18	2	9	7	12	24	31	22*	31	2	10	26	39	17	11	22
7	1	11	13	26	2	15	12	8	4	17	22	6	12	22	20
25	8	23	11	29	33	22	37*	32	9	29	11	27	5	1	9
5	4	13	29*	21	6	17	15	5	27*	37	7	21	19	12	25*
13	6	29	6	17	16	25	6	12	5	25	29	17	13	7	16
14	17	21	12	31	25	11	21*	2	6	33	25*	26	27	13	5
9	9	8	21	8	8	21	8	4	23	20	24	28	14	10	4
15	22	27	18	16	28*	23	9	20	25*	34	28*	7	34*	14	13

NASCAR/WINSTON CUP

DRIVER	POINTS	DAYTONA INT'L SPEEDWAY FEBRUARY 14		RICHMOND FAIRGROUNDS RACEWAY FEBRUARY 21		NORTH CAROLINA MOTOR SPEEDWAY MARCH 6		ATLANTA INT'L RACEWAY MARCH 20		DARLINGTON INT'L RACEWAY MARCH 27		BRISTOL INT'L RACEWAY APRIL 10		NORTH WILKESBORO SPEEDWAY APRIL 17		MARTINSVILLE SPEEDWAY APRIL 24		ALABAMA INT'L MOTOR SPEEDWAY MAY 1		CHARLOTTE MOTOR SPEEDWAY MAY 29		DOVER DOWNS INT'L SPEEDWAY JUNE 5	
		Q	F	Q	F	Q	F	Q	F	Q	F	Q	F	Q	F	Q	F	Q	F	Q	F	Q	F
1. Bill Elliott	4488	31	12	16	12	1	6	3	19*	15	4	13	1	2	10	15	11	11	7	6	19	17	1
2. Rusty Wallace	4464	5	7	4	7	6	14	4	2	5	25*	16	4	3	4	2	16	15	10	11	2	11	3
3. Dale Earnhardt	4256	6	10	2	10	22	5	2	1	2	11	4	14	10	3	14	1	16	9	7	13	9	16
4. Terry Labonte	4007	8	5	10	9	10	31*	13	4	11	23	9	16	1	1	17	4	19	4	3	9	16	12
5. Ken Schrader	3858	1	6	30	20*	5	10	9	8	1	29*	6	10	5	11	7	10	6	5	19	6	13	21
6. Geoff Bodine	3799	15	14	8	13	8	18	1	33*	4	7	3	3	13	9	5	15	13	3	2	24	4	8
7. Darrell Waltrip	3764	4	11	11	4	11	24	10	3	13	24	8	23*	18	14	6	5	2	37*	5	1	22	23
8. Davey Allison	3631	2	2	15	29*	4	9	41	40*	9	3	19	29*	20	8	26	6	1	34*	1	5	14	5
9. Phil Parsons	3630	19	3	17	30*	18	15	15	37*	19	8	7	22*	12	7	31	9	3	1	12	8	7	39*
10. Sterling Marlin	3621	12	8	14	5	14	3	11	20*	16	5	15	8	22	16	21	2	8	6	20	27	18	11

NASCAR/WINSTON CUP

DRIVER	RICHMOND INT'L RACEWAY SEPTEMBER 11		DOVER DOWNS INT'L SPEEDWAY SEPTEMBER 18		MARTINSVILLE SPEEDWAY SEPTEMBER 25		CHARLOTTE MOTOR SPEEDWAY OCTOBER 9		NORTH WILKESBORO SPEEDWAY OCTOBER 16		NORTH CAROLINA MOTOR SPEEDWAY OCTOBER 23		PHOENIX INT'L RACEWAY NOVEMBER 6		ATLANTA INT'L RACEWAY NOVEMBER 20	
	Q	F	Q	F	Q	F	Q	F	Q	F	Q	F	Q	F	Q	F
1. Bill Elliott	20	7	3	1	2	6	2	4	1	5	1	4	6	4	29	11
2. Rusty Wallace	21	35*	5	3	1	3	3	1	12	1	3	1	2	5	1	1
3. Dale Earnhardt	19	2	12	2	10	8	11	17	22	6	13	5	13	11	2	14
4. Terry Labonte	22	3	25	18	5	7	24	10	9	4	7	3	17	2	9	8
5. Ken Schrader	4	18	9	35*	19	4	7	7	3	8	21	11	24	14	7	6
6. Geoff Bodine	23	22	6	5	3	5	5	31*	8	3	20	30*	1	6	6	15
7. Darrell Waltrip	25	8	7	17	20	1	10	2	21	12	5	31*	16	13	13	5
8. Davey Allison	1	1	10	4	22	18	14	19	13	11	6	27*	20	3	23	2
9. Phil Parsons	26	24	16	14	23	21	18	27*	10	2	23	8	18	9	19	16
10. Sterling Marlin	24	16	15	23*	18	26*	9	5	20	14	18	34*	9	10	8	12

Q = Qualifying
F = Finished
* = Not running at the finish

IMSA/CAMEL GTP

DRIVER	POINTS	DAYTONA INT'L SPEEDWAY JANUARY 31		MIAMI GRAND PRIX FEBRUARY 28		SEBRING INT'L RACEWAY MARCH 20		ROAD ATLANTA APRIL 10		WEST PALM BEACH APRIL 24		LIME ROCK PARK MAY 30		MID-OHIO SPORTS CAR COURSE JUNE 5		WATKINS GLEN JULY 3		ROAD AMERICA JULY 17		PORTLAND INT'L RACEWAY JULY 31		SEARS POINT INT'L RACEWAY AUGUST 14	
		Q	F	Q	F	Q	F	Q	F	Q	F	Q	F	Q	F	Q	F	Q	F	Q	F	Q	F
1. Geoff Brabham	186	—	—	1	8	—	—	13	1	1	1	2	1	1	1	1	1	5	1	1	1	1	1
2. John Neilsen	140	6	1	3	2	5	6	1	2	4	10*	1	2	6	2	—	—	2	4	6	3	2	2
3. Price Cobb	137	3	9	8	1	2	3	15	5	13	3	13	6	2	4	3	10*	7	3	4	5	5	4
4. James Weaver	131	3	9	8	1	2	3	15	5	13	3	4	13*	1	2	6	2	7	3	4	5	5	4
5. Martin Brundle	127	6	1	3	2	3	15*	—	—	—	—	1	2	6	2	5	15*	2	4	6	3	2	2
6. Davy Jones	118	2	10*	7	6	5	6	3	4	2	2	6	3	4	3	6	12*	4	5	5	4	3	3
7. Jan Lammers	112	2	10*	7	6	5	6	—	—	2	2	6	3	4	3	6	12*	4	5	5	4	3	3
8. Chip Robinson	88	8	7	4	4	1	10*	2	3	5	9*	3	4	5	6	2	2	9	2	8	10	9	6
9. John Morton	81	—	—	1	8	—	—	13	1	1	1	—	—	—	—	1	1	5	1	2	2	6	8
10. Klaus Ludwig	78	7	4	2	5	4	1	—	—	—	—	—	—	—	—	—	—	—	—	—	—	6	8

Q = Qualifying
F = Finished
* = Not running at the finish

RIVERSIDE INT'L RACEWAY JUNE 12		POCONO INT'L RACEWAY JUNE 19		MICHIGAN INT'L SPEEDWAY JUNE 26		DAYTONA INT'L SPEEDWAY JULY 2		POCONO INT'L RACEWAY JULY 24		ALABAMA INT'L MOTOR SPEEDWAY JULY 31		WATKINS GLEN AUGUST 14		MICHIGAN INT'L SPEEDWAY AUGUST 21		BRISTOL INT'L RACEWAY AUGUST 27		DARLINGTON INT'L RACEWAY SEPTEMBER 4	
Q	F	Q	F	Q	F	Q	F	Q	F	Q	F	Q	F	Q	F	Q	F	Q	F
8	16	4	10	1	2	38	1	2	1	8	8	3	3	1	3	6	2	1	1
2	1	17	3	5	1	19	12	11	24	22	5	2	2	7	2	17	9	5	2
6	4	18	33*	9	4	20	4	9	11	6	3	19	6	5	29	5	1	2	3
3	2	5	32*	18	3	14	19	17	9	21	14	4	18	20	13	10	22*	23	8
11	20	2	9	11	6	4	8	4	20	7	1	8	10	3	12	9	21	25	11
14	34*	3	1	2	5	10	16	5	4	4	2	1	32	2	10	3	3	4	7
7	28*	9	6	4	8	1	5	10	5	1	33*	9	20	15	17	4	7	6	4
34	32*	6	5	3	35*	3	38*	12	3	3	39*	28	16	4	1	11	4	15	9
21	5	11	8	35	7	6	3	29	31*	12	11	10	4	13	20	23	19*	21	6
10	9	21	28*	15	37*	7	34*	8	14	2	6	14	8	14	11	13	12	12	5

IMSA/BARBER SAAB PRO SERIES FINAL STANDINGS

DRIVER	POINTS
1. Bruce Feldman	115
2. John Cochran	110
3. Harald Huysman	105
4. Jeremy Dale	88
5. Rob Wilson	87
6. Mark Jaremko	61
7. John Estupinan	60
8. Tom Dolan	51
9. Brian Bonner	33
10. Giuseppe Cipriani	31

SCCA/CORVETTE CHALLENGE FINAL DRIVER STANDINGS

DRIVER	POINTS
1. Stuart Hayner	795
2. Juan Manuel Fangio II	778
3. Tommy Archer	725
4. Andy Pilgrim	714
5. Mark Wolocatiuk	702
6. Shawn Hendricks	667
7. Mark Dismore	645
8. Peter Cunningham	622
9. Jim Vasser	595
10. Bill Cooper	552

IMSA/INTERNATIONAL SEDAN CUP FINAL STANDINGS

DRIVER	POINTS
1. Parker Johnstone	145
2. Amos Johnson	132
3. Doug Peterson	123
4. Dennis Shaw	89
5. Dave Jolly	85
6. Bob Strange	57
7. Lance Stewart	30
8. Bob Carradine	22
Tom Lyttle	22
10. Neil Hannemann	18

SAN ANTONIO GRAND PRIX SEPTEMBER 4		COLUMBUS GRAND PRIX OCTOBER 2		DEL MAR FAIRGROUNDS OCTOBER 23	
Q	F	Q	F	Q	F
1	8*	2	1	4	13*
3	6*	5	10	—	—
2	1	10	15	13	6
2	1	10	15	13	6
—	—	4	18*	1	1
7	2	5	10	—	—
—	—	5	10	1	1
8	7*	—	—	—	—
1	8*	—	—	—	—
—	—	19	2	6	2

CART/HFC FINAL STANDINGS

DRIVER	POINTS
1. Jon Beekuis	147
2. Tommy Byrne	144
3. Dave Simpson	122
4. Calvin Fish	113
5. Juan Manuel Fangio II	105
6. Ted Prappas	103
7. Gary Rubio	83
8. Mike Snow	70
9. Paul Tracy	58
10. Guido Dacco	53

IMSA/AMERICAN CHALLENGE FINAL STANDINGS

DRIVER	POINTS
1. Dick Danielson	90
2. Wayne Darling	52
3. Clay Young	30
Steve Clark	30
5. Mark Porcaro	22
6. Tom Forgione	21
7. Irv Hoerr	20
Craig Carter	20
9. Dennis Weglarz	19
10. John Cleveland	16

IMSA/CAMEL LIGHTS

DRIVER	POINTS	DAYTONA INT'L SPEEDWAY JANUARY 31		MIAMI GRAND PRIX FEBRUARY 28		SEBRING INT'L RACEWAY MARCH 20		ROAD ATLANTA APRIL 10		WEST PALM BEACH APRIL 24		LIME ROCK PARK MAY 30		MID-OHIO SPORTS CAR COURSE JUNE 5		WATKINS GLEN JULY 3		ROAD AMERICA JULY 17		PORTLAND INT'L RACEWAY JULY 31		SEARS POINT INT'L RACEWAY AUGUST 14	
		Q	F	Q	F	Q	F	Q	F	Q	F	Q	F	Q	F	Q	F	Q	F	Q	F	Q	F
1. Tom Hessert	163	—	—	1	1	65	13*	12	1	9	1	34	4	9	2	23	5	23	5	27	3	27	9
2. Jim Downing	108	52	1	3	2	43	1	16	15	16	9	52	3	23	6	22	3	24	3	23	4	25	7
3. David Loring	101	—	—	2	4	65	13*	14	9*	11	2	41	11	11	1	23	5	16	11*	26	7	26	6
4. Howard Katz	87	61	7*	5	6	50	2	28	4	15	4	44	10*	20	21*	22	3	24	3	—	—	28	8
5. Charles Morgan	84	—	—	—	—	64	16*	18	17*	13	16*	37	1	18	3	16	7*	14	10*	19	1	21	4
6. Martino Finotto	69	56	8	4	5	49	8	21	2	18	15*	46	5	22	11*	17	2	—	—	—	—	—	—
7. Ruggero Melgrati	64	52	1	—	—	43	1	—	—	—	—	52	3	—	—	17	2	28	13*	—	—	—	—
8. Terry Visger	55	66	14*	15	10	57	10	22	14	22	3	36	2	17	15	20	6	21	1	22	5	27	9
9. Skeeter McKitterick	45	64	2	14	25	48	7	25	10	22	10	44	10*	27	8	18	1	18	2	20	8	22	11*
10. Dan Marvin	41	65	10*	19	20*	59	3	24	5	—	—	45	6	31	13*	—	—	21	1	—	—	18	1

Q = Qualifying
F = Finished
* = Not running at the finish

IMSA/CAMEL GTO

DRIVER	POINTS	DAYTONA INT'L SPEEDWAY JANUARY 31		SEBRING INT'L RACEWAY MARCH 20		WEST PALM BEACH APRIL 24		SUMMIT POINT MAY 22		MID-OHIO SPORTS CAR COURSE JUNE 5		ROAD AMERICA JULY 17		PORTLAND INT'L RACEWAY JULY 31		SEARS POINT INT'L RACEWAY AUGUST 14		LIME ROCK PARK SEPTEMBER 5		WATKINS GLEN SEPTEMBER 25		COLUMBUS GRAND PRIX OCTOBER 2	
		Q	F	Q	F	Q	F	Q	F	Q	F	Q	F	Q	F	Q	F	Q	F	Q	F	Q	F
1. Scott Pruett	158	23	1	18	4	2	6	1	1	1	4	26	4	1	2	6	3	3	16*	1	2	1	2
2. Wally Dallenbach	114	—	—	19	1	4	17*	4	4	6	6	32	6	4	4	2	2	6	1	6	4	3	11*
3. Willy T. Ribbs	96	30	6*	21	18*	3	4	3	9	3	8*	31	3	3	9*	5	1	5	2	4	8*	4	7
4. Pete Halsmer	87	23	1	18	4	1	1	2	2	4	10*	27	2	2	1	1	11*	1	12	2	12*	2	9
5. Dennis Aase	84	31	10*	23	16*	—	—	7	3	—	—	30	1	5	3	4	4	2	18*	3	1	5	4
6. Roger Mandeville	72	21	3	28	6	8	13*	9	7	10	5	33	7	7	5	7	5	9	13*	9	3	—	—
7. Chris Cord	64	31	10*	23	16*	6	3	7	3	2	1	—	—	—	—	—	—	—	—	3	1	—	—
8. Jack Baldwin	56	—	—	33	9*	7	2	6	5*	7	3	44	10*	—	—	—	—	10	4	7	7*	—	—
9. Buz McCall	51	43	2	33	9*	—	—	6	5*	—	—	44	10*	—	—	—	—	—	—	7	7*	13	3
10. Andy Petery	51	36	4	30	3	—	—	8	8*	—	—	42	5	—	—	—	—	—	—	—	—	—	—

Q = Qualifying
F = Finished
* = Not running at the finish

IMSA/CAMEL GTU

DRIVER	POINTS	DAYTONA INT'L SPEEDWAY JANUARY 31		MIAMI GRAND PRIX FEBRUARY 28		SEBRING INT'L RACEWAY MARCH 20		SUMMIT POINT MAY 22		MID-OHIO SPORTS CAR COURSE JUNE 5		ROAD AMERICA JULY 17		PORTLAND INT'L RACEWAY JULY 31		SEARS POINT INT'L RACEWAY AUGUST 14		LIME ROCK PARK SEPTEMBER 5		WATKINS GLEN SEPTEMBER 25		COLUMBUS GRAND PRIX OCTOBER 2	
		Q	F	Q	F	Q	F	Q	F	Q	F	Q	F	Q	F	Q	F	Q	F	Q	F	Q	F
1. Tom Kendall	163	—	—	1	1	65	13*	1	1	9	1	34	4	9	2	8	8	1	2	11	1	12	1
2. Amos Johnson	108	52	1	3	2	43	1	16	15	16	9	52	3	23	6	12	4	6	14*	12	14*	15	4
3. Max Jones	101	—	—	2	4	65	13*	14	9*	11	2	41	1	11	1	11	2	3	3	13	2	11	3
4. Bart Kendall	87	61	7*	5	6	50	2	28	4	15	4	44	10*	20	21*	16	3	—	—	18	3	—	—
5. Dorsey Schroeder	84	—	—	—	—	64	16*	18	17*	3	16*	37	1	18	3	9	1	2	1	36	19*	18	15*
6. Al Bacon	69	56	8	4	5	49	8	21	2	18	15*	46	5	22	11*	15	6	8	5	17	17*	19	5
7. Dennis Shaw	64	52	1	—	—	43	1	—	—	—	—	52	3	—	—	—	—	—	—	12	14*	21	9
8. Kal Showket	55	66	14*	15	10	57	10	22	14	22	3	36	2	17	15	18	5	5	4	21	5	22	10
9. Bill Auberlen	45	64	2	14	25	48	7	25	10	22	10	44	10*	27	8	25	10	—	—	15	4	—	—
10. Dick Greer	41	65	10*	19	20*	59	3	24	5	—	—	45	6	31	13*	29	11	15	13	31	6	26	12

Q = Qualifying
F = Finished
* = Not running at the finish

266

SAN ANTONIO GRAND PRIX SEPTEMBER 4		COLUMBUS GRAND PRIX OCTOBER 2		DEL MAR FAIRGROUNDS OCTOBER 23	
Q	F	Q	F	Q	F
22	4	22	1	19	2
19	2	23	2	25	3
14	11*	22	1	19	2
19	2	31	4	26	6*
11	10*	—	—	17	4
—	—	—	—	—	—
—	—	—	—	—	—
15	8*	26	5	22	5
12	1	21	11*	14	1

DEL MAR FAIRGROUNDS OCTOBER 22	
Q	F
2	2
6	3
1	1
3	13*
5	14*
—	—
—	—
—	—
—	—
—	—

DEL MAR FAIRGROUNDS OCTOBER 23	
Q	F
1	1
7	8*
2	17*
11	5
6	3
17	19*
—	—
16	14*
4	11
20	7

IMSA/FIRESTONE FIREHAWK ENDURANCE CHAMPIONSHIP FINAL STANDINGS

DRIVER	POINTS
GRAND SPORTS	
1. Joe Varde	113
2. Doug Goad	107
3. Leighton Reese	87
Brad Hoyt	87
5. Don Wallace	86
6. Buddy Norton	76
7. Andy Pilgrim	70
8. John Stump	64
9. John Petrick	62
10. Ray Korman	56
Willy Lewis	56
SPORTS	
1. Norris Rancourt	146
2. Terry Earwood	91
John Green	91
4. Garth Ullom	89
Dorsey Schroeder	89
6. Jeremy Dale	82
7. Parker Johnstone	79
8. Steve DeBrechi	73
9. Pierre Honegger	64
David Loring	64
TOURING	
1. Paul Hacker	138
2. Alistair Oag	130
Dave Roseblum	130
4. Karl Hacker	118
5. Al Salerno	104
6. Roberto Lorenzutti	75
7. Larry Harvey	73
8. Fred Schueddekopp	61
9. John Olch	60
10. Irv Hoerr	41
Scott Hoerr	41

WoO/COPENHAGEN-SKOAL SPRINT CARS FINAL STANDINGS

DRIVER	POINTS
1. Steve Kinser	9,505
2. Sammy Swindell	9,262
3. Bobby Davis, Jr.	9,102
4. Dave Blaney	8,731
5. Mark Kinser	8,549
6. Andy Hillenburg	8,118
7. Cris Eash	7,710
8. Jac Haudenschild	7,682
9. Doug Wolfgang	7,655
10. Danny Smith	7,061

USAC/JOLLY RANCHER CANDIES MIDGETS FINAL STANDINGS

DRIVER	POINTS
1. Rich Vogler	863
2. Terry Wente	572
3. Kevin Olson	541
4. Mel Kenyon	502
5. Russ Gamester	401
6. Johnny Parsons	301
7. Dean Billings	278
8. Stan Fox	244
9. Bob Cicconi	229
10. Steve Knepper	208

BUDWEISER INTERNATIONAL RACE OF CHAMPIONS FINAL STANDINGS

DRIVER	POINTS
1. Al Unser, Jr.	66
2. Terry Labonte	55
3. Scott Pruett	51
4. Bill Elliott	46
5. Dale Earnhardt	45
Geoff Bodine	45
7. Al Holbert	39
8. Al Unser	38
9. Chip Robinson	36
10. Chris Cord	26
11. Bobby Rahal	24
12. Roberto Guerrero	19

SCCA/VALVOLINE CHAMPIONSHIP FOR BOSCH/VW SUPER VEE

DRIVER	POINTS	PHOENIX INT'L RACEWAY APRIL 10 Q	F	LONG BEACH GRAND PRIX APRIL 17 Q	F	DALLAS GRAND PRIX MAY 1 Q	F	INDIANAPOLIS RACEWAY PARK MAY 28 Q	F	WISCONSIN STATE FAIR PARK JUNE 5 Q	F	DETROIT GRAND PRIX JUNE 19 Q	F	NIAGARA FALLS GRAND PRIX JUNE 26 Q	F	CLEVELAND GRAND PRIX JULY 3 Q	F	MEADOWLANDS GRAND PRIX JULY 24 Q	F	MID-OHIO SPORTS CAR COURSE SEPTEMBER 4 Q	F	ROAD AMERICA SEPTEMBER 11 Q	F
1. Ken Murillo	194	3	1	5	4	5	4	4	3	5	6	8	3	3	2	6	4	2	4	3	1	2	2
2. E. J. Lenzi	163	6	4	22	29*	9	3	1	2	2	2	3	2	18	6	7	7	9	2	5	2	6	4
3. Bernard Jourdain	152	4	18*	2	3	2	1	5	4	7	5	2	12	12	3	3	2	3	16*	2	5	4	3
4. Paul Radisich	146	—	—	1	1	1	2	9	12	8	7	1	1	2	1	4	1	1	12*	1	3	11	5
5. Robert Groff	135	20	5	3	2	3	23	2	7	1	1	4	26*	21	5	1	3	5	13*	8	4	1	1
6. Mark Smith	108	1	16	9	5	15	6	6	6	6	8	6	22*	8	4	2	5	4	1	10	10	2	9
7. Mike Smith	90	2	17	14	8	17	13	3	1	4	3	7	14*	6	8	6	6	7	17*	4	6	5	17
8. Stuart Crow	83	14	6	24	11	14	10	10	13	9	17	11	6	5	7	9	10	8	15*	6	14	8	6
9. Jim Ward	55	10	11	25	17	21	16	14	14*	10	13	13	8	16	13	18	19*	14	7	17	8	13	15
10. Roberto Quintanilla	53	—	—	—	—	20	12	7	5	—	—	10	7	7	9	—	—	10	9	12	7	2	10

Q = Qualifying
F = Finished
* = Not running at the finish

SCCA/ESCORT TRANS-AM CHAMPIONSHIP

DRIVER	POINTS	LONG BEACH GRAND PRIX APRIL 16 Q	F	DALLAS GRAND PRIX MAY 1 Q	F	SEARS POINT INT'L RACEWAY MAY 29 Q	F	DETROIT GRAND PRIX JUNE 18 Q	F	NIAGARA FALLS GRAND PRIX JUNE 26 Q	F	CLEVELAND GRAND PRIX JULY 2 Q	F	BRAINERD INT'L RACEWAY JULY 17 Q	F	MEADOWLANDS GRAND PRIX JULY 23 Q	F	LIME ROCK PARK AUGUST 6 Q	F	MID-OHIO SPORTS CAR COURSE SEPTEMBER 3 Q	F	ROAD AMERICA SEPTEMBER 10 Q	F
1. Hurley Haywood	152	9	2	4	1	7	6	10	1	5	13	4	4	4	2	4	2	11	4	6	3	8	4
2. Irv Hoerr	141	2	5	5	2	2	2	11	18	4	3	2	2	1	5	5	7	2	3	1	8	2	28*
3. Scott Pruett	117	1	7*	6	27*	3	3	3	2	3	2	1	34*	—	—	1	3	1	1	3	16	1	1
4. Jim Derhaag	104	10	6	10	5	8	7	13	4	17	23*	15	10	5	3	14	8	12	8	8	14	15	9
5. Darin Brassfield	101	8	21*	13	3	6	9	16	38*	6	4	7	32*	6	25*	8	12	6	2	2	6	3	27*
6. Hans Stuck	100	4	29*	—	—	—	—	2	35*	—	—	3	1	3	1	2	1	—	—	5	1	4	2
7. Lyn St. James	98	7	3	18	11*	15	11	9	9	19	7	11	7	12	7	13	11	4	11	10	10	10	8
8. Les Lindley	95	3	4	7	19*	5	4	8	12*	7	5	5	3	2	21*	7	10	7	6	9	4	12	30*
9. Walter Roehrl	80	—	—	1	13*	4	5	—	—	1	1	—	—	—	—	—	—	3	5	—	—	—	—
10. Paul Gentilozzi	80	5	1	3	23*	14	8	7	3	8	17	10	5	8	4	10	4	14	32*	11	32*	13	36*

Q = Qualifying
F = Finished
* = Not running at the finish

NASCAR/CHARLOTTE-DAYTONA DASH FINAL STANDINGS

DRIVER	POINTS
1. Larry Caudill	2,552
2. Mickey York	2,233
3. Shawna Robinson	2,179
4. Todd Cray	2,164
5. Karen Schulz	2,055
6. Mitchell Calhoun	2,051
7. Tim Bender	1,923
8. James Durham	1,897
9. Scott Weaver	1,832
10. Dale Howdyshell	1,799

NASCAR/BUSCH GRAND NATIONAL NORTH FINAL STANDINGS

DRIVER	POINTS
1. Jamie Aube	2,752
2. Dick McCabe	2,716
3. Dale Shaw	2,689
4. Chuck Bown	2,575
5. Kelly Moore	2,569
6. Joe Bessey	2,251
7. Stub Fadden	2,231
8. Jimmy Burns	2,120
9. Pete Silva	2,117
10. Larry Caron	2,086

NASCAR/WINSTON WEST FINAL STANDINGS

DRIVER	POINTS
1. Roy Smith	418
2. Bill Schmitt	381
3. Chad Little	368
4. J.C. Danielsen	329
5. Hershel McGriff	328
6. Jim Bown	318
7. Bob Howard	313
8. Scott Gaylord	309
9. John Krebbs	298
10. Sumner McKnight	271

<table>
<tr><th colspan="2">PENNSYLVANIA INT'L. RACEWAY SEPTEMBER 24</th><th colspan="2">ST. PETERSBURG GRAND PRIX OCTOBER 22</th></tr>
<tr><th>Q</th><th>F</th><th>Q</th><th>F</th></tr>
<tr><td>2</td><td>1</td><td>3</td><td>2</td></tr>
<tr><td>5</td><td>3</td><td>5</td><td>4</td></tr>
<tr><td>9</td><td>2</td><td>1</td><td>1</td></tr>
<tr><td>10</td><td>8</td><td>—</td><td>—</td></tr>
<tr><td>1</td><td>11*</td><td>4</td><td>3</td></tr>
<tr><td>3</td><td>5</td><td>2</td><td>14*</td></tr>
<tr><td>4</td><td>4</td><td>8</td><td>13*</td></tr>
<tr><td>7</td><td>6</td><td>11</td><td>5</td></tr>
<tr><td>11</td><td>9</td><td>17</td><td>7</td></tr>
<tr><td>—</td><td>—</td><td>—</td><td>—</td></tr>
</table>

<table>
<tr><th colspan="2">MOSPORT PARK SEPTEMBER 25</th><th colspan="2">ST. PETERSBURG GRAND PRIX OCTOBER 23</th></tr>
<tr><th>Q</th><th>F</th><th>Q</th><th>F</th></tr>
<tr><td>6</td><td>22</td><td>3</td><td>18</td></tr>
<tr><td>3</td><td>5</td><td>5</td><td>4</td></tr>
<tr><td>—</td><td>—</td><td>—</td><td>—</td></tr>
<tr><td>13</td><td>6</td><td>9</td><td>9</td></tr>
<tr><td>2</td><td>1</td><td>4</td><td>2</td></tr>
<tr><td>—</td><td>—</td><td>1</td><td>28*</td></tr>
<tr><td>7</td><td>8</td><td>7</td><td>8</td></tr>
<tr><td>5</td><td>11*</td><td>11</td><td>7</td></tr>
<tr><td>4</td><td>4</td><td>2</td><td>1</td></tr>
<tr><td>11</td><td>13</td><td>8</td><td>26*</td></tr>
</table>

NHRA WINSTON DRAG RACING FINAL STANDINGS

DRIVER	POINTS
TOP FUEL	
1. Joe Amato	14,104
2. Darrell Gwynn	13,070
3. Eddie Hill	12,768
4. Gene Snow	10,006
5. Dick LaHaie	9,418
6. Frank Bradley	8,168
7. Gary Ormsby	7,386
8. Dennis Forcelle	6,680
9. Shirley Muldowney	5,792
10. Jack Ostrander	5,226
FUNNY CAR	
1. Kenny Bernstein	12,362
2. Mark Oswald	11,710
3. John Force	11,336
4. Don Prudhomme	10,150
5. Ed McCulloch	9,554
6. Bruce Larson	9,382
7. Mike Dunn	7,312
8. Johnny West	6,072
9. Dale Pulde	5,978
10. John Martin	5,278
PRO STOCK	
1. Bob Glidden	14,466
2. Warren Johnson	11,334
3. Tony Christian	9,822
4. Bruce Allen	9,450
5. Butch Leal	8,876
6. Jerry Eckman	8,040
7. Morris Johnson, Jr.	7,946
8. Johnny Delco	7,110
9. Joe Lepone, Jr.	6,064
10. Mark Pawuk	6,002

IHRA DRAG RACING FINAL STANDINGS

DRIVER	POINTS
TOP FUEL	
1. Gene Snow	13,860
2. John Carey	7,490
3. Eddie Hill	7,340
4. Dennis Forcelle	7,060
5. Joe Amato	6,810
6. Bill Mullins	5,680
7. Jack Ostrander	5,100
8. Richard Holcomb	4,450
9. Darrell Gwynn	4,130
10. Connie Kalitta	4,000
FUNNY CAR	
1. Ed McCulloch	14,520
2. Mark Oswald	7,890
3. Scott Kalitta	5,930
4. Dale Pulde	5,570
5. Darrell Amberson	5,400
6. R.C. Sherman	5,030
7. Doc Halladay	4,260
8. Tom Hoover	3,790
9. Brad Tuttle	3,210
10. John Force	3,150
PRO STOCK	
1. Rickie Smith	13,590
2. Warren Johnson	10,860
3. Tim Nabors	8,640
4. Terry Adams	6,370
5. Harry Scribner	6,170
6. Kenny Koretsky	6,030
7. Morris Johnson, Jr.	5,640
8. Larry Morgan	4,880
9. Jerry Eckman	4,590
10. Charles C. Garrett, Jr.	4,120

Index